This guidebook was created to draw your awareness to the pressure points that commonly leave mothers feeling inadequate and invisible.

It was also created to acquaint you with the ways in which becoming a mother can be a powerful and galvanising force in your life.

You deserve to know about both.

Infused with quotes and gentle words of encouragement, this guide illuminates the beauty and burdens of motherhood and matrescence.

Let it evoke your feminine wisdom - the rebel, the healer and the magic that lies within - so you can create your own liberated version of motherhood and matrescence.

The Journey Ahead

Exploring Matrescence	1
Mothering with Mutuality	59
When Our Mothering is Judged: Every Day Is an Audition	*83*
A Safe Harbour	*95*
The Joys of Mothering: Loving Moments, Lasting Memories	*100*
The Motherhood Realm	113
The 'Good' Mother	*126*
The Invisible Loads	*148*
Support & Self-Care	247

Welcome Beautiful Mumma

to your guidebook through Motherhood & Matrescence

Introduction

Becoming a mother is a wild and daring adventure into the unknown. It's a profound voyage of self-discovery that promises not only to alter your definition of love but to completely reshape who you are.

As you journey through motherhood and matrescence, your perception of the world - and how the world perceives you - will also undergo radical change.

Becoming a mother is a massive adjustment. You will need support - and you are worthy of it.

Reclaiming Your Body — 303

Your Body has not Failed — 310
Mothers and Mother Nature — 321
The Maternal Body: Private or Public Entity? — 335
She's Got the Look — 348
Whose Body is This? — 355
Reclaiming Sovereignty — 364

Celebrating Your Mother Tribe — 373

The Power of Storytelling — 391

– SPECIAL BONUS –

Continue your transformative journey with this complimentary journal.

SCAN WITH YOUR CAMERA OR GO TO
motherhoodandmatrescence.com/
bookbonus/

Exploring Matrescence

Exploring Matrescence

Maya Angelou famously said, *'We delight in the beauty of the butterfly, but rarely admit the changes that it has gone through to achieve that beauty.'*

The same is true of mothers.

We delight in a mother's gifts and the ways in which she loves and empowers her children. But we rarely admit the life-altering changes a woman goes through as she mothers.

Matrescence honours a woman's metamorphosis.

Exploring Matrescence

Although the term 'matrescence' was coined in 1975 by anthropologist Dana Raphael, it is only now receiving the attention and reverence of which it is worthy.

The failure to acknowledge matrescence as a normal, developmental transition means many of us assume the role of mother will neatly integrate with our to-do list.

We aren't anticipating our entire lifestyle, our thoughts, our hearts and the very essence of who we are to be altered so dramatically.

Exploring Matrescence

Similarly, most of us aren't expecting the joy and gratitude that having children brings to exist alongside the sensation of losing our self.

We become a mother thinking we know who we are and therefore the mother we will be. But our lived experience, our mothering practices and the mother we become are often very different to what we anticipated.

For many mothers, simply knowing that this disorientating period of growth is real and has a name, can bring a sense of relief and validation.

Exploring Matrescence

Before we get into the nitty-gritty, let's get clear on what matrescence is and how to pronounce it.

Matrescence, pronounced 'mæ tres . nts', is the transformative experience of becoming a mother. It encapsulates all the changes that becoming a mother brings to our life and our identity.

Matrescence is an incredible and unexpected opportunity for psychological, physical, spiritual and social evolution - a recalibration of the self.

This process is not always easy because in order to transform and transcend, the person we are and the ways in which we relate to the world must be cracked wide open.

Exploring Matrescence

Matrescence is similar to adolescence, which stems from the Latin word *adolescere*, meaning to grow, mature, emerge.

Whilst we're familiar with adolescence, we've been socialised to understand our development as complete once we reach adulthood.

Matrescence challenges this idea and asserts that becoming a mother is a universally shared transition and transformation. It unearths a new version of us. More aware. More rebellious. More empowered.

Exploring Matrescence

The journey of matrescence unfolds every time we become a mother. It doesn't matter whether we have one pregnancy or a tribe of children, and it doesn't matter whether we embrace the title of mother through pregnancy, adoption, surrogacy, family structures or birth, we will experience matrescence.

It is a sacred rite of passage that belongs to all mothers.

Exploring Matrescence

You might be wondering when matrescence begins for you. Well, that's a tricky one because the point at which matrescence begins depends on the individual.

Unlike pregnancy and birth, matrescence isn't linear. It isn't constrained by a neatly defined starting point or finish line, and it isn't aligned with the weeks of gestation, trimesters, or the age of our children.

This flexibility invites us to navigate the journey, be it our maiden voyage or another sacred cycle, at our own pace.

Exploring Matrescence

Throughout our life, we will notice that the intensity of matrescence ebbs and flows.

This is because matrescence is deeply intertwined with our cycles of menstruation, pregnancy, birthing and menopause. These cycles often oscillate us between socialisation and quiet introspection, outward growth and deep self-reflection.

Matrescence is also felt with varying intensity as we move through the early mothering stages, the storm of toddlers, the stress of teens and onwards towards empty nesting and grandparenting. Each new stage brings insights and extends our personal growth.

Exploring Matrescence

One thing is certain. Where there is change, there is growth. And when we become a mother, change is ubiquitous.

Socially, culturally, politically, financially, physically, biologically, neurologically, psychologically, morally, spiritually ...

Within us and around us, everything changes.

Exploring Matrescence

"

A new relationship with the universe.

Sexuality, politics, intelligence, power, motherhood, work, community, intimacy will develop new meanings; thinking itself will be transformed.

– Adrienne Rich

Exploring Matrescence

Everything changes. The most observable changes women experience during matrescence are the embodied transformations of pregnancy, birth and breastfeeding.

These experiences underscore the relationship we have with our maternal body. They adjust our body image, our sense of control and the trust we place in our body. They abruptly alter how our body is spoken about, who accesses it, and who believes they have expertise and authority over our body.

The respect we are shown and how we judge our physical appearance and performance during these critical events, are important. These factors influence the feelings of competence and confidence we have as we move further into matrescence.

Everything changes. What we can't see, is how matrescence transforms our brain.

The neurological transformations we experience during pregnancy and mothering are fascinating yet frequently misunderstood. The term 'baby brain' has led many people to believe that the functionality of the maternal brain is reduced.

Scientific research, however, reveals the opposite.

Neuroscientist Dr. Jodi Pawluski explains that during matrescence the maternal brain becomes more flexible, responsive and alert. Whilst it is more susceptible to stress during periods of heightened neural plasticity, it is certainly not in deficit. The maternal brain is rapidly transforming and evolving.

Exploring Matrescence

Everything changes. Becoming a mother alters our participation in creative, career and community ventures. It radically shifts our priorities, our availability, our sense of entitlement and our definition of success.

After years of fast-paced forward momentum, changing lanes to care for children can feel stifling.

Stepping back or becoming separated from an energy of productivity, which focuses on what we're going to be, do, experience and achieve next, is especially challenging in a culture that measures our worth on external achievements and accolades.

Matrescence compels us to pause and consider a new version of fulfilment, new values, a new way of living.

Exploring Matrescence

"

Matrescence is the greatest opportunity to redefine our relationship with the masculine and feminine energies within.

- Amy Taylor-Kabbaz

Exploring Matrescence

Everything changes. Matrescence reshapes our connections with other women. The level of acceptance and understanding shown towards our mothering choices and our children, will distance us from some women and weave others into our life forever.

Matrescence will inevitably shape our views of other women and women's issues. It will redefine what we believe women deserve, what mothers deserve and what we believe we deserve.

For many women, this journey prompts us to consider the experiences of our ancestral lines and become curious about our own mother's journey – in order to understand her, and our self, more thoroughly.

Exploring Matrescence

99

Our ancestors dwell in the attics of our brains as they do in the spiralling chains of knowledge hidden in every cell of our bodies.

- Shirley Abbott

Everything changes. Matrescence reconfigures every relationship we have.

Becoming a mother not only changes our availability, it prompts us to consider how healthy each relationship is for us and how aligned each relationship is with the legacy we are trying to create for our children.

Similarly, the flame we have with our partner will be tested. The way our household runs, the way we understand each other, value each other, value sexual intimacy, sleep, socialisation and support will not only change, it will be irreversibly revolutionised.

Despite the gravity of these changes, the relationship that matrescence will most greatly impact is the relationship we have with our self. We will need to unlearn and relearn who we are, and this is not a simple task.

Exploring Matrescence

"

Just as my body had stretched and ached to bear this child, so my whole life - my relationships, my ambitions, and my self image - would have to rework itself around the baby's presence.

- Nina Barrett

Exploring Matrescence

Everything changes. Matrescence not only changes how we see the world but also how the world sees us.

During matrescence, there will likely be times when your voice, your struggles, your intellect and abilities feel imperceptible to others. The totality of who we are becomes obscured by pastel-hued images of a doting mother and pervasive expectations of how we 'should' feel and behave now we are a mother.

As our mother identity takes centre stage, the woman behind the mask of motherhood becomes invisible.

The truth - that motherhood marginalises mothers and can have a lasting impact on a woman's life - is an uncomfortable aspect of matrescence we rarely talk about.

Exploring Matrescence

❞

When we celebrate the birth of a new child, we pay joyous tribute to the enlargement of the human circle. Yet with every new addition there are new subtractions (contractions) of a woman's life and range of experiences. In order to gain new life in motherhood, she must lose life.

To mask the magnitude of this sacrifice with silence, guilt, and denial is to trivialise a genuinely heroic journey into selfhood.

– Susan Maushart

Exploring Matrescence

Take a moment to reflect on your own experiences.

Had you heard of matrescence before becoming pregnant?

Honestly, did you have any idea that becoming a mum would change you in so many ways?

Did anyone tell you?

Exploring Matrescence

Most women enter motherhood entirely unaware of matrescence and the transformation that awaits them.

Makes you wonder why, doesn't it?

Can you imagine how much more agency women would have if they knew about the changes matrescence can bring?

Can you imagine if women had a shared language and could use this knowledge to understand and articulate their own experiences, to find and create the right support networks?

If women were acquainted with matrescence before they became mothers, can you imagine how much more prepared and powerful they would be?

Exploring Matrescence

Transformative rites of passage, such as matrescence, embrace three distinct stages of transition, separation, liminality, and integration.

Separation marks disconnection and detachment from aspects of our current identity and life as we know it.

Liminality represents a gateway between identities. It's in this stage that we often feel betwixt and between and experience disorientation, because we are no longer who we were, but we are not yet clear on who we are becoming.

Integration feels more certain. It's where we begin piecing our self back together. We recalibrate, observe role models and seek guidance in order to emerge more confident in our maternal identity.

This process happens over and over again. We are on a journey of growth.

Exploring Matrescence

Separation can be a daunting stage of our transition.

It represents the disconnection from familiar roles, routines and relationships. A shift in how we feel, think and act. Life is changing. We are changing and what once felt certain is not.

The stage of separation often requires traversing the darkest part of our self and the shadows cast by our ego before we can let go and reimagine life.

Exploring Matrescence

As we begin to let go, we relinquish patterns that no longer benefit us or align with who we are becoming.

We release people who invalidate our experiences and our worth.

We step away from roles and responsibilities that aren't in harmony with our maternal identity.

Often, we step back from things we love but need to set aside during this season of our life.

Exploring Matrescence

Much later in our journey, we will come to know that the space we forged in our life and identity by letting go did not become desolate or abandoned. It was, in fact, sacred and fertile ground where new perspectives, passions and connections would one day flourish. This is the gift of matrescence.

Exploring Matrescence

The idea that we will begin to separate from our identity and become someone new during matrescence feels like a paradox given the very intention of having children is to add to our life, not detach from it.

But our identity does change, and in the depths of our transition, letting go of who we are and all that is familiar to us can feel excruciating and exciting at the same time.

How you feel is important. So too is how you judge yourself because of your emotions.

Exploring Matrescence

At many junctures in our matrescence, we'll gladly welcome change.

Turning our attention to the adventure of building a family, creating memories and carrying on traditions, can bring a newfound sense of purpose and swiftly alter the meaning of life.

It can feel as though we have been bestowed with the highest honour when our children need us. There is an incredible amount of joy in being needed, nurturing and leading our family.

Exploring Matrescence

Identity evolution can also be agonising. In *Stillness Speaks*, Eckhart Tolle explains that when a form that you had consciously identified with as part of yourself leaves you or dissolves, it can be extremely painful.

It leaves a hole, so to speak in the fabric of your existence. When this happens, don't deny or ignore the pain or the sadness that you feel. Accept that it is there.

Exploring Matrescence

99

If you're on the verge of breaking let every crack show. Let every piece fall to the floor and when you're ready, piece yourself back together again. You are lore. You are magic. You are the alchemist. You are sovereign.

- Sasha Kutabah Sarago

Exploring Matrescence

In many ways, matrescence resembles a spiritual awakening.

Matrescence strips us bare. It cracks us open and forces us to look at parts of our self that we're uncomfortable with, at the childhood trauma we buried, at our inner critic - and at everything we've been told we 'should' be doing.

At the same time, matrescence evokes unconditional love. It summons our courage to heal intergenerational trauma, it rouses our inner rebel, and it connects us to the sacred and mysterious.

Exploring Matrescence

The delicate fusion of love and pain, compassion and frustration, knowing and questioning, can make our transformation uncomfortable.

With our attention, identity and energy scattered we're forced out of our comfort zone, out of alignment and into the liminal void where growth occurs.

Exploring Matrescence

"

For a seed to achieve its greatest expression, it must come completely undone. The shell cracks, its insides come out and everything changes. To someone who doesn't understand growth, it would look like complete destruction.

- Cynthia Occelli

Exploring Matrescence

The wisdom of matrescence reminds us that we are not broken. We are instead in a period of transition and transformation, shedding old energies and identities so we can step into a new light.

In the liminal space, we have the opportunity to play with our identity - to try out new perspectives, new skills, new ways of speaking, to find what feels right and what is 'acceptable'. In liminality, we are renegotiating the old and creating space for a new version of us to emerge.

In the liminal stage of matrescence, it's common to feel that we've lost our self. It's hard.

It takes time to discover, create and wait for a new version of us to grow, to emerge radiant.

Exploring Matrescence

"

'Who are you?' said the Caterpillar.

Alice replied, rather shyly, 'I–I hardly know, Sir, just at present–at least I know who I was when I got up this morning, but I think I must have been changed several times since then.'

– Alice's Adventures in Wonderland

Exploring Matrescence

Matrescence inspires us to explore and reflect on our identity. It dares us to delve into the depths of self-discovery and untangle the threads of who we are from the expectations others wrap around us.

It prompts us not only to ponder who we are, but why.

Why are you who you are?

Exploring Matrescence

Matrescence compels us to question our socialisation, to compare our self to the mother we thought we would be and the mother we think we should be.

Our inner musings drive us to contemplate our childhood, the legitimacy of the expectations we strive to meet and the beliefs we've internalised about mothers, women and girls.

By becoming more aware of and resistant to external expectations, we can begin piecing together our evolving identity, consciously aligning our self with our values and the things that truly bring us joy.

This is the work that we undertake in our journey of matrescence - awakening, reconciling, rebelling, evolving.

Exploring Matrescence

Matrescence is as much about becoming a new person as it is about unbecoming all the things people expect us to be.

It's also about letting go of who we thought we would be so we can sit in the liminal space and imagine all the possibilities of who we can be.

Exploring Matrescence

Although our emerging identity belongs to us, it is not simply what we believe about our self. Our identity is also shaped by those closest to us.

To our family, we may be the weaver of magical traditions. To our children, we may be the soft place to fall. To our friends, we may be the light and laughter.

As you journey through matrescence, take a moment to consider who you are through the eyes of those who love you. Do they see a magic within you that you're yet to discover?

Exploring Matrescence

More than any other relationship, it is the connection with our children that will most deeply and irreversibly shape our emerging identity.

The infusion of new life in our body and in our family blurs our boundaries of identity and independence, changing who we are, forever.

These blurred boundaries raise questions. Is it 'I and me' or 'we and us' now? Who are you? Who am I? Where does one begin and another end in a physical, emotional, social and spiritual sense?

These deeply existential questions are present in our day-to-day life, yet they remain unnamed, unacknowledged.

Exploring Matrescence

This book welcomes the concept of mutuality - the profound interconnection between a mother and her child - into the fields of matrescence, mothering and motherhood.

Mutuality is a critical aspect of matrescence because it honours both the 'I' and 'we'.

Mutuality seeks to acknowledge and harmonise the needs of mothers and their children at every stage of life and embeds the idea that the experiences of mothers and children are equally important.

Mutuality acknowledges that what happens to one, impacts the other, and the relationship between the two.

Exploring Matrescence

We're well-acquainted with the ways a mother shapes her children, but we seldom acknowledge that this relationship, characterised by mutual transformation, works both ways.

Mothers and their children are intricately entwined, co-creators in each other's evolution.

Exploring Matrescence

Mutuality exists during pregnancy. Everything we experience from hormones to nutrition, movement, light and sound, feeds into a field of reference for our baby.

Similarly, we are influenced by our baby's experiences. Their growth, movement and health also influence us. Their very existence transforms us. Our body, thoughts and hopes are forever changed.

Exploring Matrescence

Mutuality exists deep in the womb. Hidden from the eyes of the world, a sacred bond of mutuality entwines a mother and her baby.

As our cells play their anticipated role in nurturing our growing baby, a lesser-known marvel is also unfolding.

Cells from our baby traverse the placenta and remain part of our body for many decades. These cells enter our bloodstream and organs and even venture through the blood-brain barrier, metamorphosing into neurons that embed themselves within the intricate tapestry of our mind.

This phenomenon, if your inner geek is curious, is fetomaternal microchimerism.

Mutuality exists in the placenta. For many mothers, the placenta is the first tangible expression of mutuality. Dr Kristin Collier weaves intrigue into its very existence, explaining that as cells from the embryo reach down towards the mother's uterine wall, spiral arteries from the mother's uterus reach upwards towards her embryo.

This exclusive connection between a mother and her child is honoured in many ancient rituals and ceremonies that pay homage to the life-giving placenta.

Exploring Matrescence

Mutuality exists in labour. It is present when a baby's readiness to be born triggers hormonal changes in the mother, initiating the labour process. As the mother's contractions facilitate the baby's descent, each movement becomes a signal, a shared communication between them.

Labour is not only about the birth of a baby and the 'performance' of a mother. Above all else, it is a sacred dance between the two that is swayed by numerous biological and psychosocial factors.

Labour invites a mother and her baby to work together amid external circumstances, to push forward towards the unknown, towards separation. There is no going back. Birth is the beginning of a new self, of a new life – together, but apart.

Exploring Matrescence

Mutuality exists well beyond the early years.

Even as our children mature and their physical need for us declines, the emotions and experiences of our children remain tightly intertwined with our own. Joy, fear, success and sadness all remain interconnected. What happens to one continues to impact the other.

Embedded within matrescence, mutuality persists across our lifespan. It gently reminds us to honour our individual needs, the unique experiences of our child and the intricacies of the affinity we share.

Exploring Matrescence

❞

Until one becomes a mother, no one can ever tell you what it will feel like to love someone else so deeply and profoundly that you will rejoice when they rejoice, ache when they ache, feel what they feel - without ever speaking a word.

- Jennifer Quinn

Exploring Matrescence

The mutuality of the mother-child connection is a unique lifelong bond that will shape us in ways we never imagined possible.

There is an expectation that we will love and form a deep bond with our child, even if it's not instantaneous. What is unexpected though, are the ways in which our child will love us and how incredible this love feels.

Exploring Matrescence

Mutuality fosters a sense of belonging to something greater than our self. To the universe, to each other, to humanity. The love we have for our children often spills over into compassion for other people, for nature and all sentient beings. It brings a sense of connectedness that ushers in a new way of thinking, seeing and experiencing the world.

Have you noticed this? Have you felt it?

This paradigm shift, motivated by the most profound love, is an unparalleled privilege of matrescence.

Exploring Matrescence

Looking back, it will seem absurd to believe that the role of mother would seamlessly fit into our life and that life would remain the same. That we would remain the same.

This innocence stems from not telling women the truth about matrescence and society's peculiar transfixion with new mothers 'getting back to normal'. Subscribing to this impossibility means we'll miss the remarkable opportunity matrescence presents to evolve, to ascend and to experience our maternal identity as a powerful and energising force in our life.

Exploring Matrescence

99

Our transformation is not always loud and + arrow fast. Sometimes it's years later, you're standing there when your jaw softens and you realize, you're no longer the same as when you first walked in.

- Danielle Doby

Exploring Matrescence

Although the path through matrescence
is nuanced by our individual emotions,
experiences, herstory and perspectives,
matrescence is not solely a personal odyssey.
It is inherently political.

How our society understands and values
matrescence determines how we're supported
by our family, our workplace and our
community, in this major life transition.

Exploring Matrescence

The recognition of matrescence as a normal developmental process has the potential to shift our understanding of maternal mental health and well-being from a model of pathology to a strengths-based framework. This massive paradigm shift not only acknowledges the magnitude of change and upheaval that women experience as they become mothers but also the potential and possibilities for growth.

Exploring Matrescence

So how do you prepare for all the possibilities – the identity shift, the epiphanies, emotions and mutuality that matrescence offers?

Great question! Although we often seek stability in fixed, stratified and uniform approaches, they will likely be inadequate. We cannot prepare for something beyond our imagination with such rigid responses. Matrescence is dynamic, unpredictable, wild, surprising and energetic.

Knowledge creates a powerful foundation. Ongoing matricentric support provides a sacred space to explore your experiences, to be heard, validated and understood.

You deserve both.

Exploring Matrescence

Matricentric support should feel safe enough that you can honour all aspects of your experience – the beauty and the burden, the misery and the magic.

It should meet you exactly where you are in your journey and help you to rediscover yourself, and your power, by matching the vulnerability of matrescence with equal measures of love and acceptance.

Matricentric support should never pressure you to make meaning from your experiences of becoming. Instead, it should help you understand the process, to trust the process and not rush the process in which a woman is reborn, and a new mother emerges.

Mothering with Mutuality

Mothering - verb; the enactment of skills and the embodiment of care. A complex demonstration of responsibility, hope and love that can shape generations.

Mothering with Mutuality

At first, the term 'mothering' may seem like an exclusive term compared to the inclusivity offered by the word 'parenting'.

Parenting, however, doesn't reflect the embodied realities of mothering a child or the variances in the lived experiences and expectations placed on mothers as opposed to fathers.

Mothering with Mutuality

In recent history, mothering has been focused on providing optimal protection, resources and care to enhance a child's development. This child-centred approach is concerned with how aspects of a mother's life - her emotions, attitudes, employment, social life - impact her child's development and future potential.

This perspective, although insightful, often places the lives of mothers and their children in competition.

The child-centric view of mothering not only fails to honour the connection between a mother and her child, it also fails to consider how mothering impacts mothers.

Mothering with Mutuality

Mothering matters
to mothers as well as
children.

Mothering with Mutuality

The concept of mutuality is a healthy framework for mothering. It takes into account the individual needs of a child but extends beyond other parenting concepts by reflexively acknowledging the needs of a mother, as well as the importance of the relationship between them.

This framework doesn't sideline the needs of our children to preference our own nor does it favour the needs of our children to the point that we neglect or martyr our self. It is centred on both - together and apart.

Mothering with Mutuality

In mutuality, a mother, a child and their relationship are all equally and centrally situated.

Mothering with Mutuality

For many mothers, mutuality is a game-changer. The shared centre of mutuality challenges the patriarchal dynamics of parenting, where mothers exist primarily to provide care.

Honouring the reciprocal nature of mutuality allows us to reimagine the role of mother as an enriching force in our own life, as well as our children's.

Mothering with Mutuality

Shifting our understanding of mothering from a one-directional flow of energy - where a child is the sole focus - to a shared centre creates the opportunity to enrich the mother-child connection and to make visible the mother in mothering.

Mothering with mutuality creates space for each of us to see our self more fully and to recognise our existence and identity beyond the role of mother, whilst also acknowledging that being a mother and our mothering practices are inherently tied to our identity, our sense of self-worth and our well-being.

Mothering with Mutuality

Intuitively and intellectually, mothers have known for a long time that what happens to one, impacts the other. The concept of mutuality, which validates our individuality and our intertwinement, prompts us to question why society's understanding of the mother-and-child relationship remains so wildly different. It also leads us to question why we've sentimentalised childhood but failed to consider mothers, who accompany children in this magical stage, beyond the role of servitude.

This curiosity invites us to explore the stories we've internalised about mothers and mothering and contemplate how these narratives impact our children, our connection, our mothering and our well-being.

Mothering with Mutuality

One of the most pervasive stories we've been told is that mothering is the pinnacle of femininity and that all women, as a result of their biology, possess a deep desire to become a mother.

We've also been led to believe that upon becoming a mother, a natural maternal instinct takes hold and enables women to effortlessly carry, birth and feed their children. This maternal instinct, akin to a sixth sense, reputedly enables mothers to instantly bond with, console, and control their children.

Despite our familiarity with these ideas, they are myths.

Mothering with Mutuality

"

A myth is a kind of story told in public, which people pass on to one another. Myths wear an air of ancient wisdom, but that is part of their seductive charm... Myths convey values and expectations which are always evolving, always in the process of being found out.

– *Marina Warner*

Mothering with Mutuality

The pervasiveness of these myths and the mystical powers mothers purportedly possess, means mothering is often more complex and challenging than we imagined.

It isn't always the fairytale we're sold of love at first sight, easy connection and calm togetherness. It isn't as controllable, predictable and scheduled as baby books suggest. And it isn't always as natural, gentle and warm as mainstream media portrays.

Whilst we can never be fully prepared for the beautiful, worrisome, intoxicating, and raw experiences of mothering, these myths present such a warped view of mothering that many mothers end up feeling as though they are inadequate, and their mothering is deficient.

Mothering with Mutuality

The truth is you are enough. Your mothering is good enough.

Mothering is a skill set. Much like other skills, it takes time to learn and refine our abilities. Mothering is not just 'something women do'. It's an immersive experience that requires constant learning, contemplation and adaptation.

Mothering with Mutuality

Although many mothers experience biological and neurological adaptations that prime us to care for our children, confidence and competence in our mothering grows over time. It stems from closeness with our children, from time spent thinking about them and self-reflections about our mothering practices. The ability to mother is not a hardwired trait that is magically activated once we become mothers.

Mothering may appear instinctive or intuitive, but it is very much an intellectually reflexive and informed practice.

> I looked on child rearing not only as a work of love and duty but as a profession that was as interesting and challenging as any honourable profession in the world and one that demanded the best that I could bring to it.

- Rose Fitzgerald Kennedy

Mothering with Mutuality

Maternal skills manifest differently for everyone. Some mothers excel at hands-on practical care, some prefer play or emotional and intellectual nourishment. Some question if their ability to mother exists at all.

If we aren't fluent in the language to describe our maternal skills beyond conventional definitions, we might overlook their presence entirely. Our skills can emerge as sacred birth or family rituals. They might emerge as razor-sharp senses and a heightened awareness or perhaps a subtle, seemingly mystical synchronisation with our children.

Our skills often start as a whispering inner voice weaving together learnings, instinct and intimate knowledge of our child. As you journey forward, hold onto these whispers. Allow them to echo and amplify louder than expectations.

Mothering with Mutuality

Mothering is demanding work. It requires us to learn and carry out an extensive array of physical, emotional, social and cognitive skills to support our children's growth into well-rounded individuals.

This involves fostering a safe and supportive environment, being responsive to a child's physical, emotional, social and intellectual development, setting boundaries, instilling values and supporting them to acquire the agency and autonomy needed to navigate life.

Mothering with Mutuality

The work of mothering involves a delicate equilibrium.

On one hand, it involves celebrating our child's individuality by fostering their personal interests and unique skills. On the other, it requires us to socialise our children to be altruistic global citizens who can find their tribe, fit into society and experience a sense of accomplishment and belonging.

It sounds simple enough in theory, but the realities of mothering - the daily grind, the physical and mental toll, the bewilderment that comes from constant repetition - are anything but simple.

Mothering with Mutuality

Having a child with complex needs means mothering will also be more complex, more demanding. Similarly, mothering can be made more complex and nuanced by our own intersectionality: our race, class, gender, trauma, disability, mental health, neuro-divergency.

Mothering with mutuality in mind means that despite the silence, stigma and stereotypes, we don't lose sight of the mothers and children who sit within the margins. Their voices, reflexively amplified by mutuality, encourage us to see the breadth of the human experience and dismantle systemic barriers which fail to recognise that what happens to one deeply impacts another.

Mothering with Mutuality

Mothers, children and families can thrive when mothering is respected, valued and supported.

Mothering is an invaluable investment in the future: the most important job in the world, we've been told. The problem is, there is a lack of social respect, value and understanding of the work performed by mothers. Society takes the positive influence mothering has on individual and community well-being for granted. It also fails to recognise the time and energy needed to mother. As a result, many mothers encounter incompatible career and care responsibilities, inadequate support systems and inequitable divisions of labour within the home.

The subsequent burnout, stress and judgement negatively impact the well-being of a mother, her children, their connection and the family unit.

Mothering with Mutuality

Mothering isn't meant to be done alone.
The task is simply too big, and the joys
are simply too precious not to be shared.

Mothering with Mutuality

Rather than acknowledging the value and richness of the care work performed by mothers and embedding this significance in our culture or creating adequate supports, we find it relegated to one day of the year. Celebrated within the confines of commercial interests, the true value of mothering is whitewashed.

It doesn't have to be this way.

Mothering with Mutuality

Mothering from a framework of mutuality provides a unique way to understand and value mothering. When considering the needs of a child, mutuality seeks to make the inclusion of a mother's experiences and needs – automatic, reflexive, normal.

Consideration of a mother and her experience creates space to honour the embodiment of mothering, to make visible the invisible loads of mothering and to understand the pressures mothers experience.

Mutuality prompts us to ask, 'What is mothering like for mothers? What is it like to be a mother?'

Mothering with Mutuality

Being a mother isn't quite the same as any role we've played before.

Being a mother is different. It's not a role that we occupy between nine to five or that we can opt out of, graduate or resign from.

Once we are a mother, we are a mother in every social context we enter. And if we're really honest, most of us are unprepared for this.

Mothering with Mutuality

When Our Mothering is Judged: Every Day Is an Audition

The social environments we occupy, the stage on which we mother and the audience that is observing us have an enormous impact on how we mother, and how we feel about our self and our mothering.

In a sense, mothering is performative. This doesn't imply that our mothering is insincere, but rather it showcases the dynamic and adaptive nature of mothering.

Mothering often requires us to improvise our actions and adjust our script, tone, body language and emotional expression based on the audience and the expectations of the environment in which we are performing.

Mothering with Mutuality

Our performance as a mother is often judged according to the behaviour of our children.

It is expected children can and will be good, well-mannered and well-behaved. It's also assumed that 'good' children must have 'good' mothers.

Even though there are a multitude of factors beyond our mothering that contribute to our child's behaviour at any given moment, the pressure to be seen as a 'good' mother raising a 'good' child is real and felt intensely by many mothers.

The weight of social expectations can feel threatening and swiftly influence how we talk to, connect with and discipline our children.

The quality of our mothering performance is also measured by the success of our children.

The pressure to raise successful, happy, high-achieving children who sleep through the night, reach milestones in line with their peers, participate in extracurricular activities, attend prestigious schools, have the right clothes, jobs, attitude, emotional literacy, academic intelligence, and excel in sports and social endeavours can be immense.

It's worth considering if these measures are more reflective of personal interests, privilege and circumstance than the individual strengths of our child and the quality of our mothering.

Mothering with Mutuality

When our children are complicit with notions of success and 'good', we spare them the pain of being judged and momentarily alleviate critique of our mothering.

It's worth taking a moment to contemplate, whether in subscribing to these measures of success we place unnecessary expectations on our self and our children. And whether in striving towards these narrow, prescriptive ideals of success, we move our self and our children further from authentic self-discovery.

Mothering with Mutuality

99

We must release expectations and allow our children to evolve authentically. They will always tell us who they are if we are willing to give them space to explore. If we truly listen.

- Amethyst Joy

Mothering with Mutuality

The expectations for mothers and children are so deeply woven into the fabric of society that sometimes it takes years before we prioritise the relationship with our children above societal expectations.

Mothering with Mutuality

This can be harder than it sounds. Societal expectations about 'good' mothering are all around us, yet we rarely discuss how they can create divisions between mothers and their children. Becoming aware of expectations, and the impact they have, gifts us the opportunity to revolutionise our approach to parenting and deepen the connection we have with our children.

Often it takes heartbreak, disconnection and burnout, followed by rebellion, courage and resilience, to mother in a way that rejects notions of the 'good' child and 'good' mothering paradigms.

> By acquainting mothers with their maternal agency, authority, autonomy, authenticity, and activism, opportunity for new and broader maternal practices, beliefs and aspiration are sparked.

— Dr Andrea O'Reilly

Mothering with Mutuality

It's interesting to contemplate how we want others to perceive our children and our mothering. But the more important questions that mutuality prompts us to contemplate are how do we feel about our mothering? How do we want to feel about our self while mothering? And equally as critical, how do our children experience our mothering?

In other words, who are we mothering for?

Mothering with Mutuality

Mothering with mutuality honours the experiences of our child and our experiences as a mother, while emphasising the preciousness of the connection between us.

Mutuality is the key to mothering our child in a way they need us to and in a way that feels right for us, not in the way society or a particular parenting paradigm tells us to.

Mothering with Mutuality

"

Before becoming a mother I had a hundred theories on how to bring up children. Now I have seven children and only one theory: love them, especially when they least deserve to be loved.

– Kate Samperi

Mothering with Mutuality

A Safe Harbour

Holding space for all aspects of our child – the beautiful, the brazen, the cheeky and the challenging, the abilities and inabilities, the regulated and dysregulated – creates opportunity for their self-awareness and self-acceptance to grow.

When our children know that all of them and all their emotions are safe around us, we lay the foundations for honest and connective communication to flourish.

Mothering with Mutuality

Whilst honouring mothering as a guiding force in a child's life, the shared centre of mutuality fosters a relationship with our children that is founded on consideration, equity and respect.

Encouraging power with instead of power over, mutuality seeks to dismantle patriarchal power hierarchies, and encourage children and mothers to express their needs, thoughts, and feelings openly, knowing they will be valued and heard, not judged.

Mothering with Mutuality

Supporting a child to discover their voice, feelings, identity and strengths while contemplating our own is one of the most philosophical and reflective aspects of mothering.

Although we might wish to pause our child's development just long enough to get our own life together, the unfolding of our maternal identity alongside our child's provides us with invaluable insights. Our understanding of matrescence - the changes within us and around, the navigation of rules and expectations, the rapid period of growth and new learnings, the sense of discovering who we are and where we belong - is a gift that we can use to better understand our child and enhance the connection we have with them.

Developing the skills to connect to our children in such a way that they love to speak to us, means we can also learn to speak to them in a way that they love to listen to and learn from us.

For seasoned parents, this might sound fanciful. But our children are listening and learning even when we think they aren't. And despite their defiance or determination to learn the hard way, they will continue to seek our council and connection across the years – if they know we are willing to listen.

Mothering with Mutuality

Regardless of how old your children are, your words of affirmation and acceptance will always be a source of magic.

These gifts will stick to them like glitter for the rest of their lives.

Mothering with Mutuality

The Joys of Mothering: Loving Moments, Lasting Memories

Mothering from a place of mutuality reminds us that how our children experience and reflect on our mothering is equally important as our own feelings and reflections on mothering.

For many mothers, the paradox of time is felt deeply. Days of intense mothering can feel like watching our life in slow motion, but the years seemingly pass with more and more momentum.

Mothering with Mutuality

This reminds us of the need to take a break from the daily grind, as well as the preciousness of time and the value of soaking up moments and creating memories with our children - not just for them, but for us.

Mothering with Mutuality

The memories and moments we have with our children in their childhood, adolescence and adult lives are not only important for them, they are also meaningful and inspiring for us. They constitute a crucial component of our maternal identity, storytelling and growth.

Interestingly, we often recall our worst mothering moments with intensity and precision because they stand out from our day-to-day. Take a moment to notice your emotions and as many senses as you can in those beautiful everyday moments. The more senses we can recall, the more vividly we'll be able to reflect on those meaningful moments with our child.

Mothering with Mutuality

Mothering provides us with the unique opportunity to see the world through the eyes of our child. Experiencing things from our child's perspective opens the door to becoming enchanted with life once again. A caterpillar, a shell, flowers, leaves and rain, all suddenly hold the magic and mysteries of the universe that we had long forgotten.

Not every adult has a golden ticket to enter a child's world, but mothers do. For our children, connection through play and pretend, magic and make-believe, is golden. These whimsical and wondrously imaginative adventures - where we are free to be our self, to be light and to laugh - may be some of the mothering moments we reflect on most fondly.

Mothering with Mutuality

Mothering our children means sharing and co-creating the rich tapestry of daily life. The accumulation of our everyday experiences weaves together layers of deeply personal knowledge and connections. As we develop secret languages, inside jokes, routines and rituals, they create a mutual identity with our children.

Our collective memories become family stories that are recounted and cherished. They reinforce our sense of belonging to one another.

Mothering with Mutuality

Mothering offers us a bountiful blend of emotional, psychological and relational experiences. Watching our children grow, overcome obstacles and discover their strengths and abilities is a deeply fulfilling experience.

In mothering our children, we are gifted front-row seats to witness the human spirit showcase its incredible potential.

Mothering with Mutuality

99

It seems to take as much daring to face and name the ecstasies of mothering as it does the sorrows.

- Susan Maushart

Mothering with Mutuality

The deep joys of mothering often go unspoken, yet they transform us in profound ways. Mutuality provides a framework to explore how mothering and the relationship we have with our child reshape our inner world. Nothing can truly prepare us for the depth of love that exists alongside the daily challenges. Loving our children and being loved by them changes the rhythm of our heart forever. It redefines our definition of love.

Mothering with Mutuality

99

I remember being absolutely rocked to my core by how profoundly I could love another human being.

- Cheryl Strayed

Mothering with Mutuality

The love we have for our children is unrivalled in its intensity and purity. It accentuates the value of acceptance, belonging, diversity and inclusion.

In mothering our children, we are reminded that showing our children love is showing them how to love. It sparks a desire for our children to know they are loved exactly as they are, and a hope, that they will reciprocate this same integrity towards others throughout their life.

Mothering with Mutuality

Mothering from a place of mutuality creates the opportunity to showcase self-love and self-respect as well as respect for others regardless of gender, age, socioeconomic status, ability, race or religion.

Mutuality emphasises respect, shared power and collaborative decision-making. It blurs the margins and allows us to reimagine social systems. In many ways, mothering with mutuality is our contribution towards social equity.

It is a practice of mothering that many mothers potentially already embrace.

Mothering with Mutuality

Although mothering is a personal practice, it is intricately tied to the political and social systems that we live, love, work and mother within.

Through our words and our mothering practices, we have the opportunity to plant ideas in the hearts and minds of our children, to lay the foundations for family structures that share power and embrace mutuality.

In many ways, our mothering is an incredibly powerful mechanism for gradual social change.

Mothering with Mutuality

It might feel awkward at first to talk about the societal and generational benefits of mothering. But there is an untapped potency in mothering that deserves to be acknowledged.

It's not boastful, unfeminine or competitive to celebrate the joys and the power of mothering. Instead, it broadcasts the value that mothering brings to families, communities, and societies, and it accentuates the ways in which being a mother shapes us as individuals.

And, the question is, if mothers don't push past the awkwardness and talk about the value of mothering, who will?

The Motherhood Realm

The Motherhood Realm

Motherhood refers to the cultural, social and political systems we mother within.

This realm encapsulates the norms, myths and expectations that shape ideas about mothers and mothering, the social structures which provide support, and the political ideologies that create policies related to maternal healthcare, parental leave and childcare.

The Motherhood Realm

We can think of motherhood as a clandestine space that we enter as we become mothers. Until then, the inner workings of this realm and the secrets that lie within, remain beyond our grasp.

The Motherhood Realm

Crossing the threshold and entering this space, we are often surprised by how different motherhood is from what we had imagined. We may have been prepared for pregnancy and perhaps even birth, but rarely are we prepared for the expectations that reside in the realm of motherhood.

The on-call and selfless reality fused with the persistent 'shoulds' can leave us shocked, exhausted and scrambling to keep it all together.

The Motherhood Realm

Perhaps what is most confronting about motherhood is the realisation that being a mother isn't as simple as loving our child. The motherhood realm holds a multitude of expectations about what mothers should and shouldn't do.

The Motherhood Realm

At first, social expectations don't seem like restrictive rules. They appear as normal, natural behaviours for mothers.

Observing other mothers and listening to 'expert' advice, we often absorb expectations and unquestioningly integrate them into our to-do list.

In our desire to be the best mother we can be, we follow the rules and strive to meet expectations.

The Motherhood Realm

Over time, the rules and expectations of motherhood, pervade every aspect of our life and our identity and create multiple pressure points.

In her exploration of becoming a mother, author Rachel Cusk describes her attempts to conform to the rules of motherhood. She says, 'It was as though I had been brainwashed, taken over by a cult religion. And yet this cult, motherhood, was not a place where I could actually live.'

As pressure mounts, we're told to reach out, lean into our tribe, multitask, outsource, change how we're doing things and rise to the challenge. In reality, it's the rules and expectations eroding our well-being and our sense of equality, that need to be challenged and changed.

The Motherhood Realm

When we remember that motherhood is a space and its expectations are separate from who we are, we're gifted the opportunity to ponder how our time in this space influences our well-being, our identity, our mothering and our experience of matrescence.

The Motherhood Realm

"

As it stands, motherhood is a sort of wilderness through which each woman hacks her way, part martyr, part pioneer; a turn of events from which some women derive feelings of heroism, while others experience a sense of exile from the world they knew.'

- Rachel Cusk

The Motherhood Realm

Until we become curious about motherhood and the expectations placed on mothers, they are likely to remain invisible threads weaved into the fabric of our society, surreptitiously passed down from one generation to another through cultural, social, and gendered norms.

The Motherhood Realm

Understanding motherhood as a space that is constantly being reshaped and recreated – with each new generation, social movement and step towards equity – reminds us of the potential to rewrite the rules of motherhood.

The Motherhood Realm

"

Motherhood, it could be said, is the unfinished business of feminism.

- Dr Andrea O'Reilly

The Motherhood Realm

To rewrite the rules and renegotiate the expectations placed on mothers as the default parent, we need to piece together a shared herstory and create a language that boldly exposes the expectations placed primarily on mothers.

Are you ready to explore the realm of motherhood and imagine new possibilities together?

The Motherhood Realm

The 'Good' Mother

Many of the expectations placed on mothers stem from the 'good' mother myth.

Created from social and cultural norms, the 'good' mother myth reflects the aspirations, behaviours and emotions that are expected and deemed socially acceptable for mothers.

The Motherhood Realm

The notion of being 'good' is a motivation familiar to many women. From a young age, girls often receive subtle or overt encouragement to exhibit traits such as being well-behaved, polite, compliant, nurturing, pure, obedient, and accommodating.

Girls are often praised for being 'good girls' when they adhere to these expectations, and face criticism or negative reactions if they deviate from them.

The concept of the 'good' mother is much the same.

The Motherhood Realm

The 'good' mother is self-sacrificing. She knows she has the most important job in the world. She never complains. She enjoys this work, and it comes naturally to her. She is always well-presented, her house is immaculately organised and it runs efficiently. She buys locally and makes green choices. She is financially independent but never at the expense of her children. She is always available, kind and patient with her children. She attends and volunteers at their educational and extra-curricular activities but she's not boastful about her efforts. And she engages in self-care to ensure she can keep nourishing her family.

Sound familiar?

The Motherhood Realm

We all know the 'good' mother, even though she doesn't exist!

The Motherhood Realm

Similar to the iconic figures of the super-wife and super-woman, the good mother is a revered mythical creature.

Casting a formidable shadow, she sets the gold standard for mothering that we strive to attain and perpetually judge our self against.

Take a moment to reflect on the expectations you have of yourself as a mother.

How do you define a good mother?

The Motherhood Realm

Although the good mother isn't real, the pressure to embody her is very real and has been repeatedly connected to mental health, self-esteem, maternal well-being, stress and burnout.

The Motherhood Realm

For mothers, being good means giving. Giving life, giving birth, giving in, giving up, giving away, caregiving. Giving everything and finding more when it feels as though there is nothing left to give.

The Motherhood Realm

A key expectation for this generation of mothers is that we will direct all our physical, financial and emotional resources towards our children. The prevailing assumption is that we will either not notice or delight in the erosion of our own life in order to give our children every possible opportunity.

It doesn't have to be this way.

Reimagining a mother and her child as a team and honouring their mutuality allows us to demonstrate to our children that individual aspirations and family well-being can be harmonised.

The Motherhood Realm

After spending some time in the motherhood space, you might notice that the expectations of the good mother become more prominent in your ruminations.

I really should ... I wish I was more like you ... They must think I'm a terrible mother ... If I could just get my child to ... If I could do more, give more, know more, be more, be better, get it right, then everything would be okay. I would be okay. I'd be a good mother.

The Motherhood Realm

The problem with expectations is that they often belong to someone else, to another generation. And yet, we carry them around with us and let them shape our self-worth and our entire experience of mothering.

The Motherhood Realm

The pressure to uphold the expectations of others often prevents us from being fully present in the moment. Striving to embody everyone's definition of the good mother often forces us to protect our ego, which erodes the opportunity for empathy, responsivity and real connection with our children.

Consequently, we're less likely to mother authentically - and be who our child needs us to be.

The Motherhood Realm

If we strive to reach an ideal that isn't real, the authentic mother within us ceases to exist.

The Motherhood Realm

It's not easy to abandon the unrealistic expectations of the good mother. And often we don't want to. The desire to be recognised as a good mother and to genuinely embody that role for our children is incredibly powerful.

Mothering practices within the good mother stereotype can also feel deeply satisfying and bring a sense of purpose and pride. The problem is, that burnout and self-defeating thoughts often loom from our exhausting attempt to meet every expectation of the good mother, every day and in every social context we enter.

The Motherhood Realm

Many mothers worry that if they don't embody or strive to embody the good mother, they risk looking like a bad one. And for most of us, that risk feels like too much.

It feels like failure.

The Motherhood Realm

We've been socialised, for our entire lives, to be good.

As little girls, we swiftly learn that being 'bad' doesn't serve us well. As mothers, there is a slow realisation that being 'good' doesn't either.

This realisation is both frustrating and liberating.

The Motherhood Realm

These ideas of good or bad, should or shouldn't and right or wrong that are wrapped around mothers aren't fair, nuanced or real. They are false binaries - restrictive choices, that constrict who we are and how we mother.

The Motherhood Realm

Stepping away from notions of good and bad whilst journeying through motherhood and matrescence allows us to begin unearthing the authentic mother within.

Through our maternal awakening, we can consciously begin identifying which aspects of mothering we genuinely derive meaning and joy from and which parts we perform to meet expectations.

The Motherhood Realm

When we understand motherhood and the good mother myth, we get the chance to question, how much of who I am as a mother is silenced or staged to meet expectations? How much of my mothering stems from my values and mutuality? And how much is dictated by social norms and the systems I mother within?

> **If mothering is freed from the patriarchal institution of motherhood, then mothering could become a site of empowerment and social change.**
>
> *- Dr Andrea O'Reilly*

The Motherhood Realm

It takes practice and self-love to give up on
the idea of being perfect for everyone else
and begin the work of becoming the most
authentic version of our self.

The Motherhood Realm

Once you have become curious about motherhood, you'll never be able to go back. But you probably won't want to. Your discoveries will leave you more aware, more fierce, more expansive and more authentic than before.

The Motherhood Realm

99

The biggest surprise about motherhood was how completely and totally it changed how I look at myself, and what I believe I deserve, for the better.

- Leah Campbell

The Motherhood Realm

The Invisible Loads

One of the most liberating and infuriating discoveries within the realm of motherhood is that our maternal identity is tethered to an invisible load of expectations.

How well we manage the invisible loads often determines how we are judged, as mothers and as women.

The Motherhood Realm

The invisible loads refer to the unseen and unpaid mental, emotional and physical labour historically completed behind the scenes by mothers to ensure their home and the lives of those within it are healthy, happy and running smoothly.

The Motherhood Realm

The invisible loads mothers carry go a long way to explaining why we can feel overwhelmed and preoccupied in what is meant to be one of the most wonderful times of our life.

The Motherhood Realm

Voicing our maternal experiences of the invisible loads can feel vulnerable, but it's where we begin creating our own liberated version of motherhood.

It's how we make the invisible, visible.

As mothers work together to establish a language that articulates our experiences as a collective, we are starting to loosen the strings that tightly bind us to the invisible loads, which are more aptly shareable responsibilities.

The Motherhood Realm

Staying curious about the invisible loads at each stage of your mothering journey helps to promote balance and well-being in your life. But to be able to do this we need to dive a bit deeper and create a shared language that articulates how the invisible loads show up in the day-to-day life of mothers.

The Motherhood Realm

Let's start by separating the invisible loads of motherhood into five key areas:

- Domestic duties
- Mental load
- Always available
- Logistical load
- Emotional energy

The Motherhood Realm

As you make your way through these loads, take the time to contemplate the invisible loads you carry.

Do they leave you feeling as if your very essence is being extinguished? Are they equitable and shareable?

Do they align with your family goals, your values and how you want to mother?

Domestic Duties

Many mothers feel a sense of responsibility for the cleanliness, presentation and styling of their home.

These tasks are deeply entrenched in societal expectations surrounding femininity and have long been connected to the concept of being a good woman, wife and mother.

This ingrained association continues to shape women's mothering experiences.

The Motherhood Realm

Although there is certainly a sense of clarity and renewed energy that can come with cleaning, decluttering and organising our home, Clarissa Pinkola Estes reminds us that *'a woman must be careful not to allow over-responsibility and over-respectability to steal her necessary creative rests, riffs and raptures. She simply must put her foot down and say no to half of what she thinks she 'should' be doing.'*

The Motherhood Realm

Historically, women have performed significantly more housework than men. This trend, known as the double shift, persists even when women work full-time or are the primary breadwinner.

Of course, this isn't the case in every household, but it has been the status quo for many generations. It's predicted that the apron strings perennially tying domestic labour to mothering and femininity will take approximately 25 years to cut, even though mothering and housework are distinctly different tasks.

The Motherhood Realm

Domestic work is cooking, cleaning, shopping, washing, ironing, sorting, tidying, etc.

Mothering is parenting playing, listening, loving, supporting, teaching, guiding, advocating, encouraging, etc.

Mother does not mean maid.

The Motherhood Realm

99

I had abandoned myself out of love. They'd convinced me that the best way for a woman to love her partner, family, and community was to lose herself in service to them.

In my desire to be of service, I did myself and the world a great disservice.

- Glennon Doyle

The Motherhood Realm

Domestic duties are of course a necessity for households to function, and 'someone has to do it'. But what happens to mothers when they lose themselves and their spark in this endless spin cycle of domestic duties?

What's the cost for the next generation of families if we don't untangle mothers from this invisible load and share it equitably?

The Motherhood Realm

The time and energy dedicated to domestic duties is more often than not underappreciated, undervalued and unseen. Yet it's this very work that allows others within the household to have the opportunity to pursue leisure, lifestyle and career opportunities outside the home. It is this very work that allows the sanctuary of home to exist.

The Motherhood Realm

Home, for many mothers, is an extension of their energy field. An organised home often elicits a sense of clarity, control and tranquillity.

What seems to be invisible to others is that the work of transforming chaos into calm and converting the mess of living into the sanctuary we call home, takes enormous amounts of energy and time.

Home was never meant to steal our time and energy. It was meant to be a place to spend time and re-energise.

The Motherhood Realm

"

… the unwaged condition of housework has been the most powerful weapon in reinforcing the common assumption that housework is not work, thus preventing women from struggling against it, except in the privatized kitchen - bedroom quarrel that society agrees to ridicule, thereby further reducing the protagonist of a struggle. We are seen as nagging bitches, not workers in struggle.

–Silvia Federici

The Motherhood Realm

Whether we are striving towards an equitable distribution of domestic duties in our home or assuming primary responsibility for them – it will require work.

The question becomes, what do you believe you deserve, and what work is best for you in this season of your life?

The Motherhood Realm

Believing, truly believing, that mothering can exist independently of a picture-perfect home, takes time.

During maternity leave or longer absences from the paid workforce, many of us see domesticity as our contribution. Over time, this pattern becomes the norm. This is what we see mothers do. This is what we've been primed to do as young girls, good girls and good wives.

Motherhood, is the final piece of the puzzle. Cleanliness and organisation symbolise good mothering and we find solace and space in it too. It all seems to make sense, so we tie the apron strings a little tighter.

The Motherhood Realm

More food to cook, clothes to fold, towels to pick up for the fifth time this week. Toys to be put away, laundry to be washed, sinks to be cleaned, bottles to be washed, rubbish to be taken out, lunchboxes to be filled. Maintenance to be done, floors to be mopped, shopping to be done, dishwasher to be unpacked, more food to cook!

Domestic duties are like noxious weeds invading every free space, popping up in places you least expect. No matter how often you tend to them, they reappear in record time, making it impossible to gain satisfaction in finishing the job.

Strangely, no one else seems to notice them.

The Motherhood Realm

This endless and invisible cycle of domestic duties that are tied to 'good' mothering often makes women angry.

If we harness it, this anger can be our alchemy and ignite a search for agency and authority in our lives.

The Motherhood Realm

"

My home is filled with toys and noise, it has fingerprints on every wall. My hair is usually a mess and I'm always tired, but there is always love and laughter. In 20 years my children won't remember the house or my hair, but they will remember the time we spent together and the love they felt.

- unknown

The Motherhood Realm

Often when a woman refuses to be dutifully attuned or perfectly happy maintaining an immaculate household it's assumed she's not coping.

What's more likely is that she has realised that the presentation of her home has nothing to do with her competence as a mother or her personal fulfilment.

In many ways, it's a rebellion against societal expectations, and a bold assertion that her worth and the connection she has with her children transcend conformity to domestic perfection and the societal definition of 'good'.

The Motherhood Realm

99

Maybe Eve was never meant to be our warning. Maybe she was meant to be our model.

- Glennon Doyle

The Motherhood Realm

Mental Load

The mental load of motherhood involves knowing where everyone and everyone's things are at any given time. It entails making decisions, meal planning, and mentally rehearsing schedules to ensure each day flows smoothly and everyone's social, emotional and physical needs are sufficiently met.

It not only encompasses remembering and meeting everyone's immediate needs but also anticipating their future needs and desires.

The Motherhood Realm

The mental load of motherhood means mothers are always thinking twice - each decision weighed up for our self and our child. Have you noticed this, your mind engaged in a constant dialogue between your needs and feelings and those of your children? This not only highlights the mutuality that exists between a mother and her children, but also the invisible energy required to mother.

The Motherhood Realm

As mothers, our mind is constantly being inundated with internal reminders. Each mental memo urges us not to forget the myriad of tasks and responsibilities essential to our household and family.

The Motherhood Realm

For mothers, as the default parent, the mental load negates the opportunity to experience stillness.

The Motherhood Realm

Make time for stillness.

Practice listening to your intuition.

Listen closely.

She is in the stillness,

in the space between your breaths.

The Motherhood Realm

The borderless and enduring nature of the mental load means you'll likely find yourself making mental memos about your family's needs anytime, anywhere.

This perpetual state of mental alertness is an invisible load that can impact our romantic relationship, our physical and emotional well-being, our mental clarity and our ability to live in the moment.

The Motherhood Realm

You deserve to switch off.

The Motherhood Realm

When we transform our mental memos into physical lists, calendars and rituals, pressure from the mental load can begin to recede.

Making the invisible load visible, means this work can be shared, enacted and supported by others who are invested in the well-being of our family.

You don't have to carry this alone.

The Motherhood Realm

Sharing the mental load with others, including older children, can be less challenging when we create regular family rituals of communication and connection. The following questions offer a place to begin creating your unique family rituals.

What are your sources of stress at the moment?

What are the commitments of our family this month?

Is there anything we want to opt out of?

How can each of us take action?

In what ways do each of us need support?

What are our options for support?

The Motherhood Realm

Always Available

The pressure to remain physically, emotionally and mentally available to our children is a complex challenge. A number of sources contribute to this: the needs of our children, the love we have for them, the 'good' mother myth, fear of judgement, guilt, social comparison, and the systems that we mother within.

The pressure to always be available to our children weighs heavily on mothers.

The Motherhood Realm

Our availability and responsivity are most commonly motivated by the fact that we want our children to know they are loved, heard, seen, and valued. We want to nourish them, be there for them when they need us and embody the mantra of do no harm.

We want desperately not to fail them.

The Motherhood Realm

Sometimes, if we're being completely honest, our availability and attendance is motivated by the fear that our mothering will be judged negatively if we're absent. But generally, the desire to always be available to our children throughout their life exists because we don't want our children to miss out - or to miss out on our children.

The Motherhood Realm

Despite our best efforts, our ability to remain available and respond attentively to our children will be diminished by the demands of daily life.

There is a constant tension that exists, between the demands of life and the desires of and for our children to be mindfully and attentively responded to.

It's unlikely that we'll relieve this tension by continuing to believe mothers can do it all. And yet, most of us try to do more, be better, work harder and faster in order to relieve the pressure.

The Motherhood Realm

The good mother narrative leads us to believe we can do it all. It deceptively implies that we should always be able to prioritise our children, attend every event, accompany them to every extra-curricular activity, and spend endless hours playing each day - all whilst maintaining a career, a tidy house, thriving friendships and a wildly romantic relationship.

The reality is, they won't all bloom in the same season.

The Motherhood Realm

When our children are little, days seem to dissolve in a cycle of feeding, changing, soothing and playing. Life can feel like a blur as the day shift slips into night shift and around again. Countless hours are dedicated to doing everything necessary to ensure their comfort. Our responsivity teaches our children that they are safe with us.

The Motherhood Realm

As our children age, the pull to remain available changes, but it doesn't diminish. Through the school years, our availability will likely revolve around social, educational and extracurricular endeavours. The tween, teen and adult years begin to shift our availability from a constant presence to constant readiness - always available to pick them up, to pick up the bill, to pick up the phone, and to pick up on what they need from us as they navigate their own evolution. Our responsivity teaches our children that they have support.

The Motherhood Realm

The longing to continue to enrich the lives of our children is a positive force in their lives. But the level of intensity and constant availability portrayed by the good mother, isn't sustainable for one person. You don't always need to be available to create a healthy environment in which your child can thrive. Grant yourself the freedom that comes with knowing this.

When we aren't immediately available to our children, it can create manageable, tolerable and age-appropriate opportunities to model problem-solving skills, turn-taking, resilience to disappointment and consideration for the needs of others.

The Motherhood Realm

Let your heart be filled with the knowledge
that what you are doing is enough.

The Motherhood Realm

For many mothers, the idea of not always being available is paralysing. The love we have for our children, coupled with their vulnerability and the pressure to be a good mother who is always available, makes it challenging.

And sometimes, the uproar that is created by focusing on our own needs - whether for solitude, a career, socialisation, or a bathroom break - can make it feel pointless to try.

The Motherhood Realm

Mutuality reminds us that the melody of our own life needs to be heard to create a beautiful harmony with our children.

You don't always have to be available. There's more than one way to show up for your children, more than one way to mother, more than one thing that can fulfill us and more than one way to let your children know you love them.

The Motherhood Realm

The availability of mothers is commonly critiqued in the debate between 'working' mothers and stay-at-home mothers.

The duality between stay-at-home mothers and mothers engaged in paid employment is unmerited. All mothers are working mothers and each of us will experience pressure in a nuanced way to remain constantly available to our children.

The Motherhood Realm

Some mothers will face judgement for going back to work or enjoying their career, others will face judgement for being a stay-at-home mum or wanting to stay home. Some will face judgement for using daycare, others will face judgement for not using daycare.

Many will not have a choice, but will crave it.

The Motherhood Realm

There's often an expectation, that after a certain period of leave, mothers can and will effortlessly return to work. However, the lived experiences of mothers reveal this is a much more complex experience than we are led to believe.

The reality is, becoming a mother can change our priorities overnight. The trade-off between financial security, career aspirations, and being with our children can suddenly come into question in ways we never expected.

The Motherhood Realm

If you've been taught for your whole life that women can do anything, be anything, that we have power and choice, and that we can have it all, it's not hard to see why motherhood elicits feelings of inadequacy.

Suddenly doing it all feels like we need to become two people.

The Motherhood Realm

99

'But it's no use now … to pretend to be two people! Why, there's hardly enough of me left to make ONE respectable person!'

- Alice in Wonderland

This tension is further explained in Dr Sophie Brock's concept of the care career conundrum. It depicts a mother in the middle of two opposing forces.

On one side, we have the paid labour market, which measures achievement in terms of career progression, individual accolades and forward momentum. It promotes productivity, measurable output, fiscal returns, and constant availability to ensure paid work comes first so that we never 'let the team down' or miss opportunities for individual success.

On the other side is the role of the mother, who is expected to be selfless, put the needs of others first, and always prioritise the needs of children and family over paid work commitments. Success is measured by how present we are, how much we give, how 'good' our children are and how well their needs are being met.

The Motherhood Realm

If you're wondering what happened to the mother in the middle.

The Motherhood Realm

Well, she is often forgotten, and feels as though she is losing herself.

The Motherhood Realm

You cannot always be available to everyone else.

You deserve to be available to yourself.

The Motherhood Realm

99

It is tempting to believe that all mothers wake up feeling fresh every morning, never raise their voices, only cook with organic food, and are equally at ease with the CEO and the PTA.

- Jodi Picoult

The Motherhood Realm

This pressure to have a career, to be a focused, goal-orientated, always available paid worker and simultaneously the always available 'good' mother makes us vulnerable, and not because women aren't capable of mothering and working.

But because the systems that we mother within are broken.

The Motherhood Realm

The idea that we can have it all, that we can always be available to our children, stirs a sense of individual inadequacy and elicits questions about our ability.

Why is this so hard for me? Why can't I get it together?

How is everyone else doing this so well?

Am I the only one struggling?

> In a sane society no woman would be left to struggle on her own with the huge transformation that is motherhood.

— *Germaine Greer*

The Motherhood Realm

There is nothing wrong with you or your mothering.

There never was.

It's the systems that we mother within. They are not designed for mothers.

The Motherhood Realm

The patriarchal system in which we mother often assumes women are unreliable, unavailable and unable to perform their role once they become a mother. It assumes that mothers, instead of fathers, will cut back their workforce participation and by default, perform the majority of parenting and domestic labour. It assumes all mothers want to and all fathers don't.

The systems we mother within, which have historically offered both parents little flexibility to participate equitably in raising their children, are responsible for the gender pay gap, a significant number of mothers being overqualified for their paid roles or experiencing financial insecurity, and the tendency to calculate whether daycare is worth it using a mother's earnings alone.

This stark reality highlights inequalities ingrained in our society, which shape our maternal experiences.

The Motherhood Realm

Surely that's not right? Surely it's not meant to be like this?

There has to be a better way.

Listen to that!

It's your inner voice nudging you towards the version of motherhood that you envisage, towards fewer opposing forces in your life, towards equity.

> The movement away from patriarchal motherhood is not a movement away from connectedness, responsiveness and attunement with our children. It is a move towards it.

— *Dr Sophie Brock*

The Motherhood Realm

When we see that the systems we mother within entrench gendered parenting roles and prevent mothers and fathers from participating equitably in their families and the workforce, we begin stepping into our power.

The desire to do it differently sparks the search for agency.

The Motherhood Realm

You are capable of anything, you can do anything, be anything, provided you're within a community, workplace, home and family that supports you and respects the fact that there are multiple dimensions to your life.

The Motherhood Realm

Whether you're an expectant, new or seasoned mum contemplating your care or career options, remember, it's always your prerogative to search for agency and change your mind, over and over again, to strike a balance that honours the mutuality between yourself and your child.

The Motherhood Realm

Logistical Load

The logistical load refers to the physical and organisational tasks that keep a family running. It's the daily 'doing' work that maintains your household. It encompasses the scheduling, coordination and execution of each family member's activities, responsibilities, desires and needs.

This can include getting everyone ready and dropped off at daycare, school or work; preparing for and attending appointments, birthday parties and extracurricular activities; shopping for household supplies, school projects, gifts for the kids, their friends and teachers, your partner, their family and your own. Oh, and don't forget the pets!

The logistical load is the infamous 'juggle'.

The Motherhood Realm

A pivotal part of the logistical load involves responding to unforeseen circumstances such as emergencies or illness.

Mothers seem to magically appear when their children need them, but behind the scenes, they are negotiating and navigating a complex web of responsibilities to create a stable, nurturing and responsive environment for their families.

This work is invisible and often masked with a warm smile.

The Motherhood Realm

> **It takes all the running you can do, to keep in the same place. If you want to get somewhere else, you must run at least twice as fast as that!**

— Alice Through the Looking Glass

The Motherhood Realm

The logistical load, which has been equated to a full-time job - with regards to the financial worth it carries and the time it requires - can significantly impact the workforce participation and financial stability of mothers.

Constantly being on the go can also leave us feeling physically, emotionally, and cognitively depleted.

Don't underestimate the benefits of sharing these responsibilities with others committed to your family's well-being.

You are not meant to live only in the moments that exist between looking after everything and everyone else.

The Motherhood Realm

The first step to sharing the logistical load is ensuring everyone is aware of its existence.

The second is holding the belief that this work belongs to families, not just mothers.

When family life operates with seamless efficiency, the logistical load remains invisible. The thought of pausing so that it becomes visible to others is alluring, but facing the mess and disorganisation that will prevail is frightening enough to keep us in perpetual motion.

The Motherhood Realm

Sharing the logistical load can feel less challenging when we create opportunities for regularly planning and sharing gratitude with our partner, family or support circle.

A weekly ritual might include the following reflections.

What was difficult this week? How can we do it differently? When did you feel supported?

What are our family logistics this week?

How can we work together to support each other?

What support do you need this week? What support is available to us as a family?

The Motherhood Realm

Emotional Energy

The emotional energy required to mother is enormous. That's not to say that being a mother isn't rewarding. It is.

It's just a more complicated energetic exchange than most of us expect.

The Motherhood Realm

Becoming a mother elicits a new emotional load.

Not only are we navigating a new range of experiences with each child and each new stage of parenting, we're also journeying through matrescence and the state of flux that comes as our lives, our body, our relationships and our identity are rearranged.

As if feeling all the feels that come with being a mother wasn't enough, we're also reconciling how we feel against how we expected to feel and comparing our emotional experiences to how others expect us to feel.

The Motherhood Realm

The emotional energy needed to navigate mothering, motherhood and matrescence is immense.

There will be so many times when your energy radiates brightly. You'll likely feel joyous contentment when you notice alignment unfolding in your mothering, your relationships and your work. The existence of your children will remind you that you are blessed, and their faces will have an unparalleled ability to light up your world.

There will also be days, weeks, maybe even seasons when your energy recedes. You'll likely question if this is all there is, if your effervescence will ever return .

It will.

The Motherhood Realm

As mothers, a substantial amount of our emotional energy is absorbed in the mix of worry and wonder elicited while contemplating our child's well-being.

As the default parent, mothers are often held responsible for identifying and meeting children's social, emotional and physical needs.

Feeling responsible for a child's success, things that go 'wrong', or might go 'wrong', in a child's life, creates a lot of pressure for mothers. This invisible load underpins the enduring question mothers ask themselves — have I done enough?

The Motherhood Realm

You are enough. You are doing enough. Give the love you have. It is enough.

Mothers also frequently bear the responsibility of creating a positive household energy characterised by camaraderie, cooperation and polite communication.

This invisible load creates an unrealistic pressure and adds to the emotional load mothers carry.

As a result, it's often mothers who expend a significant amount of energy learning, teaching and practising skills to cultivate a positive energy within the home despite the fact that family dynamics are not solely the responsibility of mothers.

Even when armed with time, energy, skills and strategies, mothers cannot summon mystical powers to control the emotions, behaviours and interactions of their children.

We can only work to create stability and safety for these behaviours and emotions to be experienced, expressed and experimented with.

The Motherhood Realm

Remember, being a good mother doesn't mean you can control your kids or that they'll always exhibit exemplary behaviour. Watch how your energy changes when you free yourself from this illusion.

The Motherhood Realm

Fostering an atmosphere where our children can openly experience emotions and practice their social skills requires us to manage our own feelings, empathetically embrace theirs, and effectively engage in co-regulation.

This process not only demands a considerable amount of practice but also a signature blend of intellectual, physical and emotional energy.

Despite the weight and complexity of the emotional load, mothers are expected to remain positive. This is an enduring quality of the 'good' mother who is completely fulfilled by the experience of mothering.

This idea that mothers are the pinnacle of happiness and will embrace each challenge with a joyful exuberance is as mystical as the good mother. Feeling anything less than joy towards our maternal experiences - and then having to mask these feelings to appear perfectly peachy - adds additional layers to the emotional load mothers carry.

The Motherhood Realm

> **My mind dealt exclusively in internalised reprimands of how I 'should' be feeling and dark comparisons with how I was.**
>
> – *Jamila Rizvi*

The Motherhood Realm

Have you noticed that even on the toughest days you're expected to find the silver lining, to be grateful and soldier on?

This places a significant emotional burden on mothers. It tells us our feelings are wrong and compels most of us to mask the complexities of our experiences. It doesn't have to be this way.

The Motherhood Realm

Acknowledging the full gamut of emotions that becoming a mother elicits can stir a sense of vulnerability. Negative emotions aren't exhibited by the 'good' mother, meaning sadness, frustration and anger quickly become taboo.

Many women swear they'll never be 'that' angry, exhausted or worrisome mother. Until they are. Until they enter the motherhood realm and experience its challenges and complexities firsthand.

The Motherhood Realm

99

It's harder than you think to admit your even occasional dissatisfaction as a mother without feeling instant guilt, an immediate sensation of shame for even suggesting you might not be happy when you've got a wonderful healthy child…but it's not realistic or healthy to deny the fact that a mother is a complicated person—or to deny that a mother is a person at all.

- Andrea J. Buchanan

The Motherhood Realm

How much you love motherhood does not reflect how much you love your child.

Take a moment to reflect on this. There is freedom within.

The Motherhood Realm

In the chaos and charm of the child-rearing years, our sensory system is working incredibly hard to process a constant stream of sounds, smells, touches, tastes, sights and movements.

We are often running on broken sleep, jumping between work and family commitments, and trying to keep our romantic relationship and friendships afloat.

With our body, mind and heart all brimming with stimulation, our sensory system can easily become overloaded.

The Motherhood Realm

It's not uncommon for mothers to feel touched out, overstimulated, overwhelmed or nearing the edge of their flight, fight, fawn or freeze responses. These sensations are the warning signs our brain and body give us when they need respite, stimulation or soothing.

The next time you find yourself nearing tears, frustration, anger or overwhelm check in with yourself.

Have you reached your sensory threshold? What is it that your body and mind crave?

The Motherhood Realm

Patience, calm, stillness, novelty.

So many experiences can feel out of reach whilst navigating the labyrinth of motherhood. Constantly on, always responsive, alienated from our body, domestic drudgery, repeating instructions and the same processes day after day, powerful and yet somewhat powerless to take control of our days, our career, our life.

Boredom, frustration, sadness, anger, guilt.

Love, gratitude, warmth, joy, all swirling in a way that hardly makes sense.

The Motherhood Realm

There is a threshold to what the body and mind can manage and mask.

It's often unexpectedly, in the moments when we desire equity, to finish a sentence, or to feel in control of our life and our body, that a wave of emotion surges forward and words spill out. Unfiltered. Untamed.

The Motherhood Realm

Since we're talking about emotions, can we talk about anger for a minute? Because that's what often spills out.

Just to be clear, anger and abuse are fundamentally different. Anger is an emotion commonly experienced by humans – including loving mothers. Sometimes we direct it towards our self or our children because we are the only constants available to absorb the intense frustration coursing through our body. Feelings and expressions of anger, are often followed by shame, guilt, sorrow, sadness and a promise to our self and our children to do better.

Does this sound familiar?

For many mothers, it will.

The Motherhood Realm

The similarities in the emotional experiences of mothers are enlightening. They compel us to look beyond the individual and ask why.

It is perhaps a rite of passage to realise that our anger isn't meant for us or our children. It is meant for the systems we mother within. It's for the gender biases, for all that we couldn't do once we became mothers, and for the ways expectations have manipulated the relationship we have with our partner and children.

The Motherhood Realm

Our anger is valid.

If we continue to hide our anger and 'negative' emotions, the significant lack of social support for mothers and the failures of the systems we mother within will continue to remain hidden too.

The Motherhood Realm

When children witness our anger, it can be complex to process. We would be livid if anyone spoke to our children venomously, handled them roughly or caused their faces to lower in sadness and their bodies to retreat in fear.

And yet, there will likely be a time we find our self here - the bully, the perpetrator, in a moment we wish we could erase. For us and for them.

On those days, it's important to find empathy and compassion. No other job is more demanding on your body, mind and soul than mothering and navigating motherhood. It calls for patience, forgiveness, empathy and unlimited love for our children - and our self.

The Motherhood Realm

Children witnessing our full emotional repertoire - our humanness - is an opportunity to share with them the importance of emotional regulation and self-care, the process of rupture and repair, and the range of emotional experiences that exist in between linear models of sadness and happiness.

The Motherhood Realm

When we consider that we are navigating motherhood, matrescence and a newfound mutuality, it makes sense that we'll experience various levels of stress, worry, sadness, disenchantment and fatigue, along with overwhelming joy and gratitude.

But this doesn't mean that we should grin and bear it until we come out the other side, back into the 'real' world.

Motherhood and matrescence aren't a blip in reality. This is the real world, your every day, your mothering legacy and your well-being we're talking about.

It's important. You are important.

The Motherhood Realm

Next time the words and emotions spill out, listen closely. Honouring, instead of ignoring the needs and emotions that emerge during moments of overload and overwhelm can completely transform the relationship we have with our self and our children.

However, most of us aren't acquainted deeply enough with self-care or having our maternal experiences validated to embrace this process. We're more familiar with a cycle of smothering our needs and emotions with embarrassment, guilt and shame and then alleviating these feelings by dedicating more of our time and energy to others.

This self-defeating cycle can be changed when we remember to honour mutuality and talk confidently about the wide range of emotions that we've experienced.

The Motherhood Realm

Many of us have grown up with the notion that happiness represents perfection and is our sought-after destination.

But we're not one-dimensional. We can't only exist within positive emotional and behavioural states. Mothering itself requires us to have grit and grace, strength and softness, to be boundless and boundaried, resilient and rebellious.

Give yourself permission to experience all the emotions. Anger, sadness and frustration are important and can co-exist alongside joy, fulfilment and lightness.

Happiness and perfection are not the prerequisites for being loveable.

The Motherhood Realm

It's okay not to default to positive. It's okay to not know how you feel.

It's okay to feel everything or nothing.

It's okay to experience positive and negative emotional spheres at the same time.

Stand in your authenticity and every version of you will be loveable.

The Motherhood Realm

As mothers, we have a choice - expend energy masking the breadth of our emotional experiences for the benefit of others or channel it towards authenticity.

When we embrace the idea that all emotions enrich our life, and that the dark allows us to have gratitude for the light, we begin to step towards a new and profound authenticity. From this place of authenticity, our confidence grows, and we become empowered to create meaningful change that makes our maternal experiences more rewarding and joyous.

The Motherhood Realm

The biggest challenge we face as mothers is recognising that we're not just 'having a baby' or raising kids.

We're providing unpaid, high-quality care and working through all the social expectations and gendered biases that reside in the jungle of motherhood.

As if that wasn't enough, we're also experiencing the physical, social, political, emotional, behavioural, psychological and spiritual transformation of matrescence.

This requires a phenomenal amount of energy.

The Motherhood Realm

If you can, steal away time for yourself to journal or reflect on your maternal experiences and the emotional repertoire they've elicited.

Explore and be curious about your interiority – your personal thoughts, feelings, and experiences that only you have access to. It will help you move towards knowing yourself more deeply and understanding what brings you joy.

The Motherhood Realm

The benefits of finding sources that elevate and renew your energy as you navigate motherhood and matrescence cannot be overstated.

The aim is not solely to recharge so you can continue caring for your family, the aim is also to welcome a flow of joyous, uplifting, and nourishing energy into your own life because you deserve this.

Energy works best when it flows, in and out. Regularly replenishing your energy means becoming aware of your needs, acting on them and learning, possibly for the first time, to deeply value yourself and the benefits of support and self-care.

Support & Self-Care

Support & Self-Care

Support and self-care are practices, systems, and offerings that promote physical, mental, social and emotional well-being.

Support & Self-Care

For many people, maternal support conjures an image of a heavily pregnant woman or a new mother with a baby in her arms.

These iconic images highlight that we've been socialised to believe support is normal and 'acceptable' in the early stages of mothering but once we've reached the magical six-week mark or our kids are at school we should have it all figured out.

This simply isn't realistic.

Support & Self-Care

The age of our children and their proximity to us shouldn't dictate the support we receive or feel entitled to.

Seeking support as a mother is often harder than we anticipated. The 'good' mother myth tells us we should be able to do it all. It fosters the belief that other mothers are doing it all - effortlessly and unaided.

What we don't see is how other mothers are managing. We don't see if they're outsourcing domestic support or sharing the load with their tribe. We don't see the gargantuan pile of laundry or late nights making lunches and catching up on work. We don't see the whole picture, yet we tell our self to do better.

Support & Self-Care

Seeking support, although it can feel like an admission of inadequacy, is more aptly a positive and intelligent move towards individual well-being and family connectedness.

Support comes in all different shapes and sizes. It's family, it's your mother tribe, it's your partner, it's paid services who step in and step up - without imposing guilt.

It's flexible workplace policies, mother-friendly public spaces, funded childcare and community services motivated by inclusivity and family well-being.

Support also exists in language. It's in the stories of mothers, social media, academia and social movements that voice the lived experiences of mothers and aim to dismantle the notion that juggling it all is just what 'good' mothers do.

Support & Self-Care

'Why didn't you just ask for help?'

Watching the face of a mother when someone asks this question is insightful. Their appreciative nods mask an inner knowing that offers of support, although well-meaning, are also complex.

It often feels easier just to go it alone, because strangely, support has the potential to add to our mental, emotional and logistical loads.

Regular, routined and reliable sources of support, however, can reduce the invisible loads and create consistent space in our life.

Support & Self-Care

Space.

To breathe. To create.

To rest. To live.

Support & Self-Care

Seeking support is perhaps most difficult when we require it to engage in self-care.

For many mothers, self-care feels selfish. The good mother myth tells us that being absorbed in our own interests means our children are missing out.

Self-care isn't selfish; it's living.

Self-care honours the mutuality between a mother's well-being and that of her child. It shows our children that caring for our self and caring for others are not competitive forces. They are deeply connected practices.

Support & Self-Care

Amidst the chaos of the child-rearing years and reminders to 'lean in or reach out', most mothers will find self-care slips to the bottom of the list.

Releasing our self from the pressure to always prioritise the needs of others requires a considerable shift in thinking.

To regularly engage in self-care, we need to re-centre our self in our own life and truly believe that our experiences matter - that we matter - as much as our children, our family, our home.

Support & Self-Care

I matter.

I matter. I matter.

I am important.

I matter!

Support & Self-Care

Self-care is often seen as an individual responsibility.

An indulgent luxury afforded to a mother every so often so she can return to her children feeling reinvigorated and replenished. But are these short bursts of self-care really all that mothers need?

The current understanding of self-care conveniently diverts attention from the systems that we mother within. For mothers to feel deeply nourished, we need to broaden our definition of self-care and include conversations about motherhood and matrescence, the invisible loads, the pull between paid work and care work, the disparity between school holidays and the availability of annual leave, childcare costs and the gender pay gap.

Self-care is private and it's political too.

Support & Self-Care

99

It is justice, not charity, that is wanting in the world.

- Mary Wollstonecraft

Support & Self-Care

Embracing self-care is a form of activism against societal norms that value mothering over maternal well-being.

Support & Self-Care

At its core, self-care is about nurturing and restoring the relationship we have with our self. Often this requires reacquainting our self with the belief that we are worthy of our own time, energy and care.

Support & Self-Care

You deserve support. You are worthy of love, help, guidance, experiences, nourishment, space to think and time to rest.

Support & Self-Care

Essential to the practice of self-care is self-respect.

When we recognise this, we can begin to contemplate what depletes and drives our sense of self-worth. What motivates us or prevents us from engaging in self-care?

It's these questions that often bring women face to face with the mythical good mother, with the life experiences and social conditioning that shaped our sense of self-worth and control.

Self-respect is powerful.

It paves the way toward agency, authority and long-term self-care.

Support & Self-Care

If you remember one thing about self-care let it be this: self-care isn't only about filling your cup so you can continue to care for others. It's about emotional, physical and energetic nourishment because you are worthy.

Support & Self-Care

You are worthy.

You always have been.

When you deeply believe this, it will be the most decadent elixir for life.

Support & Self-Care

Self-care and support involve setting boundaries.

Boundaries are physical, emotional and psychological parameters designed to protect individual well-being and promote healthy relationships.

Boundaries define expectations and acceptable behaviour and delineate where a person's rights and responsibilities begin and end.

Support & Self-Care

Boundaries are commonly thought of as a negative term associated with toughness and inflexibility.

But setting boundaries isn't rude or controlling. In fact, it requires a delicate blend of assertiveness, awareness and attunement to the perspectives of others. Setting boundaries often means acknowledging the desires of others whilst choosing to honour your own needs, values and well-being.

This can feel incredibly uncomfortable, because from a young age, we're taught to prioritise the needs of others.

Support & Self-Care

I hope you have the courage to choose yourself.

Support & Self-Care

"

It took me quite a long time to develop a voice, and now that I have it, I am not going to be silent.

-Madeleine Albright

Support & Self-Care

The beauty of setting boundaries is that when you start saying no or voicing your needs and expectations, you define the standards by which you want to be treated.

Boundaries are a sign of your self-worth. They reflect the optimism of how you envisage your life unfolding. They allow you to protect the time and energy you want to invest in yourself and your family.

Don't be afraid to set them.

Support & Self-Care

Cues that we need to reassess boundaries can include guilt, anger, pressure to meet competing commitments and a sense of disconnection from our self or our children.

Take time to notice how you are feeling amid the chaos and charm that mothering brings.

Do you feel in control of your life? What's creating a sense of pressure? What's working for you at the moment?

Where are your feelings, time and energy invalidated?

Do you need boundaries to nourish yourself or your family?

What can you press pause on? What do you crave right now?

Support & Self-Care

Reframing boundaries as self-honouring and family-honouring choices can radically alter how entitled and empowered we feel to make decisions, without guilt.

Support & Self-Care

Self-care and support involve tuning in to our inner voice.

An important part of self-care that we don't often talk about is managing the voice in our mind.

Our inner voice, also referred to as self-talk, is the internal dialogue that guides our thoughts and decisions. It is deeply intertwined with our self-perception and emotions, and accompanies us as we problem-solve, catastrophise and fantasise.

Support & Self-Care

Our inner voice is a blend of conscious, logical reasoning mixed with deeper, subconscious symbology and stories. It reflects cultural, social and family narratives we've heard, replayed and reshaped over time.

We can hear our inner voice as clear directives, conversations, storytelling, ruminations, encouragement or soothing self-talk. It can be harmonious, scolding, determined and dissonant all in the same day.

Support & Self-Care

Most of us are so conditioned to the presence of our inner voice that we don't give it much thought.

It's familiar, it's constant. It sounds like us, so we trust it.

This familiarity often prevents us from filtering out unhelpful information, fact-checking or stopping loops of criticism and self-doubt.

Support & Self-Care

99

Be careful how you are talking to yourself because you are listening.

- Lisa Hayes

Support & Self-Care

Thinking about your own ruminations, who else's words and expectations are playing on repeat?

Self-care involves making sure what we're listening to is nourishing. This means being intentional about the sources of information and influences in our life: what and who we allow to shape our thoughts, beliefs and perspectives.

Support & Self-Care

If the influence of another is going to live rent-free in your heart and mind, then the effect it exerts, should at the very least uplift you, inspire you and champion you.

Support & Self-Care

What words do you need to hear today?

Support & Self-Care

The internal dialogue we maintain with our self possesses profound potential. It's a transformative instrument capable of shaping the contours of our psychological landscape.

Its influence is contingent upon deliberate decisions to harness its power and constantly guide it in ways that nurture our well-being.

Support & Self-Care

Curiosity and awareness have the potential to transform our mind from an echo chamber to a wonderland where compassion, creativity and growth can flourish. They help us recognise when our inner voice is going to need firm redirection or is best left untethered to discover new possibilities.

Over the next few days, take time to check in on your thoughts.

Is what you're saying to yourself healthy and helpful? If not, try reframing the conversation.

What is going well?

What is one small way you can make a positive change?

What personal strengths have you drawn on before?

Is what you're saying to yourself true? Who might have a different perspective?

Support & Self-Care

Self-care and support involve self-acceptance.

Self-acceptance is the practice of recognising our self fully and continuously cultivating a non-critical attitude towards our body, identity, our emotions, our past experiences and our interiority.

This is deep work.

Support & Self-Care

I AM ...

These are two incredibly powerful words. What you put after them shapes your reality.

Support & Self-Care

On our journey through motherhood and matrescence, the importance of self-acceptance becomes more obvious.

The challenges and changes we face will force us out of alignment into the liminal void and cause us to bloom in ways we never expected. The process of growth and the pressures of motherhood will also cause us to question how much we like who we are becoming.

Upon discovering parts of our self that we aren't comfortable with or have difficulty accepting we have choices.

Bury them, deny them and layer them with shame and silence, or unpack them, understand why they exist and learn from this.

Support & Self-Care

Growth is not a neatly wrapped gift.

It's the crumpled paper and tangled ribbon that children delight in and adults discard.

Support & Self-Care

Anyone who has grown – mentally, socially, spiritually, emotionally – knows that growth is not always comfortable. It can be equally confusing and confronting for others to witness our metamorphosis.

As your romantic relationship ruptures and repairs, as your friendships recede and reshape, and as you continue to co-create connections with your children, remember to care for yourself.

It helps.

Support & Self-Care

Although focusing on self-care, self-acceptance and personal growth can feel a little self-indulgent, the truth is - the most powerful relationship we have is the one we have with our self.

When we're comfortable with who we are and the idea of growth and 'imperfection', we're better equipped to extend this perspective, imbued with empathy, patience and acceptance, to others.

Support & Self-Care

99

To accept ourselves as we are means to value our imperfections as much as our perfections.

-Sandra Bierig

Support & Self-Care

To reach the sanctuary of self-acceptance, we must traverse the void - the uncharted liminal space between identities.

True self-acceptance is not only about feeling completely satisfied with who we are, it's also about accepting that at times we must sit in the mud with our evolving self and acknowledge that every iteration of us is worthy.

It's amid this acceptance that we come face to face with the magnificence of our muddied self. She is a perfect blend of light and dark, old and new. She's a version of us that emanates beauty, authenticity, rawness - humanness.

Support & Self-Care

Support and self-care involve time.

The intentional use of time to focus on our needs and interests is essential for welcoming self-expression, inner peace and vitality into our life.

Without it, we are unable to live life fully.

Support & Self-Care

You are already a great mother.

The task now is creating space in your life for you.

Whether you need space to ground yourself or freedom to seek out what makes you come alive, responding to your needs will allow your unique identity to flourish and your effervescence to return.

Support & Self-Care

Interestingly, small, unexpected moments of time alone, although valued, can pull even the most relaxed woman into a spin. Do we rest, clean, organise, finish a craft project, shop, shower alone, eat properly, exercise, sleep, book appointments, return the 341 calls and emails?

What am I going to do first? What do I even enjoy now?

The eagerness to indulge in an array of experiences means snippets of time for self-care can be paralysing.

Support & Self-Care

For mothers, some of the greatest barriers to self-care are the invisible loads, expectations, a lack of regular and reliable support, impossible mothering standards, and the undervaluing of our own needs.

You deserve time to move, soothe and rest your body, to nurture the intellectual, emotional, creative and spiritual aspects of the mind.
To reflect, dream, connect, laugh and ground yourself in mother-centred support.

Regardless of what you choose, you deserve regular time - for you.

Support & Self-Care

One of the greatest gifts you can give yourself and your children is the belief that we are truly worthy of our own time, energy and care.

Support & Self-Care

It can be difficult to find time for self-care amidst the competing demands of family life.

Self-care, however, doesn't have to compete with family life. In some seasons of life, self-care won't be able to be done separately from our children. Reframing self-care to include participating in activities we enjoy with our children opens up a range of new possibilities for self-care and connection.

Support & Self-Care

If time and space are elusive right now, welcome the daily practice of self-compassion and self-acknowledgement into your life.

Do something for yourself, every day.

What you do and where you do it doesn't really matter. It's the ritual of self-care that's important. Daily self-care rituals say I matter - every day.

Support & Self-Care

Support and self-care involve rest.

Rest, in case you've forgotten what it feels like, is a state of relaxation, cessation of activity, and freedom from physical, cognitive and emotional exertion. Rest is essential to replenish energy, rejuvenate the body and declutter the mind.

Support & Self-Care

In a culture that glorifies productivity and achievement, rest can feel like a guilty indulgence.

Rest is not lazy. It's an essential tonic giving your mind time to wander, your soul time to speak and your body time for respite.

Support & Self-Care

The interesting thing about rest is that you not only need it during the most challenging moments of mothering, motherhood, and matrescence; you need it once the storm has passed too.

When your body finally experiences stillness, silence and safety, it may repeatedly ask you to stop and let it rest and repair.

Support & Self-Care

The intelligence of nature doesn't lie. If your body says it needs rest, listen.

What do you need, to give yourself permission to rest, to heal and to revitalise?

Support & Self-Care

99

'Women's bodies are like the earth. Not only in their ability to give life and nourishment, but also in that they need to be gently cared for and cultivated.

- Louise Erdrich

Support & Self-Care

There is an undeniable likeness between a mother's body and Mother Earth.

Both are a source of love and nourishment, not a resource to be exhausted and depleted.

It is up to us to distinguish between the two and honour the necessity for rest and recovery.

Support & Self-Care

I am grateful for my body,

all it has done,

all it can do and

all it will do,

after I rest.

Reclaiming Your Body

Reclaiming Your Body

Reclaiming your body is a process. It's a combination of learning to honour, trust and listen to your body. It's about exploring what it means to live in your body and it's about reconnecting with your body so you can unshackle her from societal expectations.

Take your time to move through all the waypoints in this chapter; it is longer than others. It goes deep and ventures into uncommonly charted waters.

Reclaiming Your Body

In the lifelong relationship we have with our body, becoming a mother will likely be the most profound, awe-inspiring and confronting physical transformation we will have to reconcile.

Regardless of how you became a mother, as you journey through motherhood and matrescence, the way you perceive your body, talk to it, value it, present it, deprive it, allow it to be touched and hear it talked about, will swiftly be called into question.

Reclaiming Your Body

No one tells us this, but becoming a mother is one of the greatest opportunities to redefine and renegotiate the relationship we have with our body – and to reclaim it for our self.

Reclaiming Your Body

Unfortunately, in-depth conversations about how we're adjusting – psychologically, spiritually and socially – to our maternal body are few and far between. In fact, conversations are more aptly comments such as: 'You're carrying high', 'You look like you're about to pop', 'You've bounced back quickly.'

Even prenatal and postnatal appointments, which observe and inspect our body, rarely put any emphasis on the relationship we have with our body. Yet this relationship is central to our well-being. It influences how we care for our self, our sense of control and vulnerability, our decision-making, our identity and how we feel about our self as a woman and a mother.

How do you feel about your body?

Reclaiming Your Body

Historically, women's bodies have been surrounded by contradictions.

On one hand, the story of Eve constructs our bodies as impure and corrupt, a source of temptation that needs to be controlled and punished. On the other, the female body is seen as sacrosanct, pure, intuitive and in need of protection.

Motherhood and matrescence bring these subconscious psychic conflicts into our consciousness, into our body.

Reclaiming Your Body

Many of the contradictions surrounding the female body play out in the 'good' mother myth.

According to this myth, a good mother's body is naturally ripe, ready to reproduce and care for children. Despite being constantly available to her children, the body of the good mother remains neatly presented, respectably covered and unchanged by the role of mother.

The difference between the idealised maternal body and the experience of women who have embodied their power and vulnerability, is so complex to reconcile alone that it often elicits feelings of confusion, anger, guilt and inadequacy for many mothers.

Your Body has not Failed

The good mother myth perpetuates the belief that a woman's reproductive journey should be uncomplicated. The good mother's body is fertile and functional. It possesses the ability to naturally and effortlessly conceive, carry, birth and breastfeed.

How closely a woman's body meets these mythical ideals can shape whether she feels a sense of achievement and awe towards her body or a sense of frustration and failure. This is especially so when we are surrounded by terms that impart a sense of inadequacy - failure to progress, geriatric mother, incompetent cervix, failed VBAC, lactation failure, habitual aborter, insufficient supply.

This is the environment in which our maternal body image is meant to thrive.

Incompetent, failure, insufficient. These are things your body is not!

Reclaiming Your Body

Although the good mother myth draws our attention to the performance of the maternal body, what we should be focused on is how the maternal body is cared for.

The care a woman receives during her reproductive experiences and mothering years reflects how much her physical, emotional and psychological needs are valued and respected. It tells her a great deal about her worth in society.

Reclaiming Your Body

Women's bodies are diverse.

Women's reproductive experiences are diverse.

Women's emotional, physical and spiritual responses to their reproductive experiences are also diverse.

There are no 'shoulds' when it comes to your body and your experiences.

Reclaiming Your Body

This idea that our body should perform in a certain way, that it's mind over matter and that our reproductive experiences are caused solely by our body is incredibly damaging.

Our body exists within a complex web of influence. The expectations we have of our body, our history of trauma, how safe and central to decision-making we feel, institutional rules, expert power, our nervous system, the physical environment, the people around us, our baby, all these things and more, shape our maternal reproductive experiences. Most of them are beyond our control.

Reclaiming Your Body

There is nothing wrong with your body.

There never was.

It's the myths about women's bodies that need to be fixed.

Not you.

Not your body.

Your body has not failed.

Reclaiming Your Body

Your body has not failed.

Pregnancy can be a wondrously transformative experience. Sensing the powerful life force of our child within, witnessing the expansion of our body and recognising that nature's innate intelligence has taken over, can foster a deep connection and a profound sense of awe towards our body.

Pregnancy can also leave us feeling disconnected from our body. Rashes, stretch marks, pigmentation, uncompromising constipation, uncontrollable vomiting, sensitivity to smells, ninja kicks from within, back pain, restless legs and weight gain can leave us feeling as though we are a tourist in a body that is no longer familiar, a hostage in a body we can no longer control.

Reclaiming Your Body

Your body has not failed.

Birthing can be addictive and intoxicating. Power and strength emerge full force; courage and determination pervade our body, and a primal instinct urges us forward. Untethered and uninhibited, a woman is connected to her mind, her body, her baby, the universe. Embodying the power of them all, she is euphoric.

Birthing can also be a time of exceptional vulnerability. The lack of control over our bodily functions and behaviour, combined with the power of institutional practices and policies, can create a profound sense of uncertainty and disempowerment. It's as though one's spirit, body, and baby are at the mercy of forces we cannot command. Long after childbirth, a woman may be taunted by her experiences. She bears physical and emotional wounds, energetic and spiritual scars.

Reclaiming Your Body

Your body has not failed.

Breastfeeding can be an incredibly connective and rewarding maternal experience that offers mutual physical relief. Not only is it an excellent ruse to get our baby back in our arms, but it's also a beautiful ritual for co-regulation, a precious moment to marvel at the exquisiteness of our baby and our body.

Breastfeeding can also be incredibly frustrating and heartbreaking. The pressure to breastfeed exclusively and enjoy it, despite the searing pain, repetition and constant tethering to another can be overwhelming. Add hungry cries and judgmental eyes and it's the perfect formula for feeling as though we're letting our child down.

Reclaiming Your Body

Your body has not failed.

Mothering creates infinite opportunities for coregulation. By adjusting our tone, volume, movement, breath and expressions we can use our body as an anchor to regulate our self and our child. In moments of togetherness and touch - whether it's imaginative play, running errands, reading stories or cradling our children as they drift towards sleep - our body can imbue a sense of calm in our children and help synchronise our heartbeats.

Mothering can also elicit dysregulation. The constantly interruptible on-call nature of mothering, coupled with a barrage of sounds and stimulation, loss of independence and the invisible loads can quickly burden a mother's sensory system. Over time, our body becomes susceptible to unparalleled levels of physical, emotional and cognitive fatigue.

Reclaiming Your Body

It's not women's bodies that have failed.

It's the expectation that our body will perform according to set timelines. It's the expectations of the 'good' mother myth that it's all going to be effortless and come naturally. It's the impossible ideals of beauty, the disregard for mutuality, the patriarchal systems we mother within, and the disinterest in a woman's relationship with her body that have failed us.

Reclaiming Your Body

Your body is doing its best. She has given you all that she has.

Be gentle with her.

She has been with you through it all and will be with you until the end.

Reclaiming Your Body

Mothers and Mother Nature

One way to enhance the relationship we have with our body is to expand our perspective of her.

At its most fundamental level, our body is part of Mother Nature. A wildish, life-giving force; a complex nexus of ancient matter; an ecosystem of energy and evolution.

Shifting our focus away from external standards of performance, beauty, and desirability creates the opportunity to turn inwards and acquaint our self with the vibrant and vital magic of Mother Nature that is inherent in our very existence.

Reclaiming Your Body

Mother Nature and the human body are inextricably connected.

Everything around us and within us is composed of elements that were forged in the hearts of ancient stars. Their explosion scattered stardust across the universe, providing the building blocks of life. The atoms in our bodies - the calcium in our bones, the oxygen in our lungs, the iron in our blood - all have stellar origins.

This profound connection anchors our body to the universe and its bedazzling cosmic expanse. Gaze upon the stars, marvel at their luminance, and be enchanted. We are all wondrously formed from stardust.

Reclaiming Your Body

By unlocking new perspectives, simple truths are illuminated. Not only is the female body formed from ancient matter, it is also a sacred site of maternal lineage.

The egg that each of us develops from was formed by our mother whilst she was within our grandmother's womb. In other words, the fortitude, well-being and adventures of our maternal line are woven into our very being.

Knowing that the strengths and resilience of our matriarchal lineage already reside within us is a beautiful awakening to the connection we have with the generations that are before us, after us, and within us.

Reclaiming Your Body

99

'Through my grandmothers' lineage, I carry stories I've never been told.'

– Linda Hogan

Reclaiming Your Body

We may not give it much thought until we become a mother, but the female body possesses an incredible intelligence.

Without our directive, Mother Nature initiates a sequence of events that transform our body: hormones surge, ligaments expand, fluid is retained, tissues soften, and skin stretches endlessly to accommodate our burgeoning belly.

Mother Nature also imbues us with the ability to nurture life and collaborate with our baby. The sharing of cells, the transfer of energy and the collaborative building of organs that takes place without conscious control is remarkable.

Reclaiming Your Body

The innate intelligence of our body reveals that we don't simply exist within Mother Nature, we are Mother Nature.

Reclaiming Your Body

Seeing our self as part of Mother Nature reveals the seasonal rhythms that reside within us.

Each season invites us to appreciate the energetic shifts our body encounters. Winter represents seasons in our life that call for deep contemplation. It is a time for turning inwards, grieving and rest. Spring symbolises freshness, new beginnings, growth and optimism. It is a season of possibilities and playfulness. Summer welcomes the infusion of vibrant energy. It is centred on celebration, connection and sharing our gifts with those around us. Autumn signifies transition. It is time to harvest our efforts and embrace abundant joy, whilst also letting go of what no longer aligns.

Becoming attuned to the seasonal rhythm of our body allows us to respect our energetic ebbs and flows and work in harmony with them.

The seasonal rhythm of our body also appears in our menstrual cycle. Winter, symbolising the bleed, offers time to turn inwards, to slow down, sleep and dream. It's during this part of the cycle that women are most likely to acknowledge themself as an integral part of Mother Nature.

Spring represents the follicular phase, where the body starts preparing for a potential pregnancy. Released from the winter, it's a time of new enthusiasm for the outer world, heightened ambition and increasing efficiency.

Ovulation is synonymous with summer. It's characterised by bright, concentrated energy, increased socialisation, connection and confidence. Love and harmony are bountiful; people are drawn to this full energy.

Reclaiming Your Body

The luteal phase, symbolised by autumn, is a time of transition and change. During this phase, a woman's inner world is often characterised by a fiery energy. She is wildly aware of everything. A decreased tolerance fused with increased sensory perceptions spurs the need for letting go, solitude and silence. This phase can also be marked by the inclusion of lively inspiration and determination to change the status quo.

The menstrual cycle is a powerful reminder that our body possesses nature's cyclic energy. By connecting with these primal and ancient forces we can align with our rhythms and use them as strengths.

Reclaiming Your Body

Your body is a sophisticated and versatile communicator.

As an extraordinary multitasker, she processes the input from eight sensory systems simultaneously. Taste, touch, sight, sound, smell, pain, temperature, balance, position, movement and interoceptive input are integrated into cohesive messages. A delicate fusion of chemical messengers, electrical impulses, organs, bone and muscle communicate throughout the body.

She also speaks the universal languages of love and laughter and converses through colour, music, movement, dance, tears, emotions, expressions, imagery, memory and imagination. Consciously and unconsciously, she is fluent in them all. Can you feel her?

Reclaiming Your Body

One of Mother Nature's most decadent gifts, with unrivalled communicative prowess, is the feminine intuition. With lightning-fast speed, she reads the energetic and emotional landscape within us and around us and helps us discern what feels 'right' before rationale can even be applied.

Bridging the known and unknown, she interlaces real-time information from our sensory system with the ancestral wisdom and instinct buried deep within our body.

Although feminine intuition is often dismissed as superstition, this internal guide reminds us of what we want and what we deserve. She is often behind closed doors, beckoning to us, reminding us to reconnect with our self, to love our self.

By listening to our intuition we not only protect our body, but the mind and psyche too.

Can you hear her?

Reclaiming Your Body

Our society rarely honours the female body as part of Mother Nature, as a sacred site of maternal lineage, or its innate intelligence and feminine wisdom.

Seeing our body as part of Mother Nature is a privilege many of us unveil by becoming a mother. Opportunities for paradigm shifts of this magnitude are rare and yet we have it right here: pregnancy, birthing, mothering and matrescence each provide a portal to this deeply nourishing and affirming perspective.

To see our body as part of nature is to embody infinite miracles and wisdom in action.

Reclaiming Your Body

The privilege of seeing our body as part of Mother Nature can mark the beginning of a new relationship with our body.

It allows us to shake up the status quo, to rediscover the body we've been inhabiting for years and experience her wisdom unconstrained.

What would happen if instead of telling our body how she should look, perform and feel at any given moment, we let her speak? What if she spoke - and we listened?

What would a world where women are well-acquainted with their wildish nature and had intuitive relationships with their body even look like? How would it feel?

How connected to your body do you feel?

Reclaiming Your Body

> When women reassert their relationship with the wildish nature, they are gifted with a permanent and internal watcher, a knower, a visionary, an oracle, and inspiratrice, and intuitive, a maker, a creator, and inventor, and a listener who guide, suggest, and urge vibrant life in the inner and outer worlds. When women are close to this nature, the fact of that relationship glows through them.

–Clarissa Pinkola Estes

The Maternal Body: Private or Public Entity?

Although the relationship we have with our body is the most important, it's certainly not the only relationship our body encounters. Overlaying the frameworks of motherhood and matrescence, it becomes clear that our body is not only a personal entity, it is a social entity too.

The places and spaces we enter and the roles we play - child, mother, woman, wife, partner, patient - influence how others access our body, feel entitled to access our body, and how they assess the appearance, value and performance of our body.

The social relationships our body conducts can significantly impact the relationship we have with our body, how we feel about it and how we feel about our self, as a woman and as a mother.

Reclaiming Your Body

Becoming a mother dramatically alters the way others relate to our body, and this is especially evident during pregnancy.

There is something alluring and captivating about the pregnant body, of seeing someone at the precipice of a new adventure, that draws people towards a pregnant woman.

Pregnancy seems to have an almost magical ability to dissolve conventional physical and conversational boundaries. Strangers and acquaintances alike can feel compelled to share their experiences, offer advice, touch your belly, and ask intimate questions about your pregnancy and impending birth.

Whether you perceive this shifting boundary as an opportunity to tap into an oracle of feminine wisdom or as an infringement on your boundaries, it's ultimately very personal and nuanced. There is no right or wrong.

Reclaiming Your Body

Pregnancy, with its inherent mutuality, blurs the bounds of our identity. People are not only connecting with us, they're also connecting to our child, through us.

Our body can suddenly feel as though it not only belongs to us, but also to our baby, our partner, our family, with their hopes and dreams for the future, our care providers, who remind us of all the things we should and shouldn't be doing, and strangers who enquire about how we're planning to birth our baby.

For many women, this can feel like a profound loss of individual identity. Our personal needs and desires are erased and replaced. We can feel as though we are only a vessel. A chalice for life.

Reclaiming Your Body

Understanding how family, friends and others relate and feel entitled to relate to a pregnant woman and her body is at the heart of body ownership and boundaries. If a woman feels as though her body has become akin to community property, where everyone is entitled to have their say, it can significantly alter her sense of authority and agency in decision-making processes.

Reclaiming Your Body

When making decisions that involve our body, we can find our self influenced by social conditioning. The 'good' girl, who is taught to acquiesce to authority and prioritise the needs of others, primes us to do the same thing as mothers.

The 'good' mother myth entrenches this ideal further by telling us that if we want the best for our child, in pregnancy, birth and beyond, we should adhere to 'expert' advice.

This deeply ingrained expectation suppresses a woman's interiority, her physiological responses and intellectual ruminations related to her decision-making.

Reclaiming Your Body

Making decisions that involve our body is rarely a simple process of yes or no; sign on the dotted line. It's an embodied process, a complex internal debate, that impacts us physically, emotionally and socially.

Given the sheer number of decisions to be made regarding conception, pregnancy, birthing and beyond, it can feel as if our body, our child's well-being, and the perception of us as a 'good' mother are constantly on the line.

Reclaiming Your Body

The good mother, who unquestioningly follows expert advice, is also a good patient. She dutifully checks her dignity at the door and submits to whatever is necessary, because that's what good mothers do, right?

The truth is, whether a woman chooses to follow 'expert' advice or undergo any kind of procedure, vaccination or examination, it has little to do with her qualities and abilities as a mother.

It's more aptly a reflection of how safe she feels, her experience of trauma, her instinct, her intellectual curiosity, who she considers an expert, and her desire to protect her body, her child and their mutuality.

The expectation that good mothers will submit their body to experts, creates a deep discomfort in many women. It often arises from a collision between the social narratives we've internalised as girls and those we've learnt as mothers.

In a society that strongly emphasises the appearance and sexuality of the female body, yet demands it be covered up to remain 'good', a conflict between modesty and motherhood is inevitable.

Reclaiming Your Body

As girls, we are taught that although our body is valued for its beauty and desirability, it must remain untouched, covered and private. As mothers, our bodies are viewed as vessels. Not sexual, desirable or private, they are suddenly subjected to being inspected, touched, shaved, cut, measured, weighed, poked and prodded.

As girls, 'good' means keeping our body protected and hidden, as mothers, 'good' means lying back and spreading your legs. The stark difference is impossible to ignore. We feel it deeply.

Reclaiming Your Body

Our decision-making is further complicated when the maternal body is pulled into competitive narratives such as the natural vs medical model of maternal health.

How each of us views natural products and treatments and the systems in which medical professionals work is not the problem. The problem is, when these views are seen as right or wrong, good or bad, it becomes contentious for mothers to be curious about their options.

A system based on false binaries creates unnecessary pressure for mothers to choose sides and then vehemently defend their position. In doing so we miss out on the breadth of knowledge and care that we are entitled to.

Reclaiming Your Body

Whether it's trying to swallow the delightful blood sugar elixir without gagging, a stretch and sweep, taking a supplement or medication, having a flu shot, weighing in, considering inductions, antibiotics, vaccinations, pain relief and caesareans, the competing paradigms that surround the maternal body and the mythical good mother who always follows expert advice go a long way to explaining the stories of mothers who feel like they didn't have much choice .

At a minimum, you deserve to be informed, and physically, socially and psychologically safe when making decisions.

Reclaiming Your Body

Making decisions that involve our maternal body is a complex process that often overlooks our interiority, our intellectual curiosities, the mutuality we share with our child and the relationship we have with our body.

By bringing awareness to expectations embedded within the good mother myth, psychic conflicts, and competing paradigms surrounding women's bodies, we can begin moving towards a more embodied decision-making process.

We can ask our self: how are expectations impacting me? What does my body need? What am I feeling? What is my body telling me? Who am I doing this for? Do I feel respected? Is my baby and our mutuality being honoured?

Reclaiming Your Body

99

It has taken me a long time to find a relationship with my body that works - one that makes me feel strong and worthy rather than ashamed.

- Emma Stone

She's Got the Look

You won't be surprised to know that the good mother myth suggests the appearance of a mother's body reflects her virtues. Women are unfortunately well-accustomed to being judged on their looks. According to the myth, the body of a good mother is pure, well-presented and appropriately covered. It's fit, healthy and well-rested because she prioritises her appearance and makes time for self-care.

This reinforces the idea that a mother's values and virtues can be discerned by how closely her body aligns with societal beauty standards.

Reclaiming Your Body

The truth is, the appearance of a woman's body and how hard she tries to adhere to beauty ideals have very little to do with her mothering values. It does, however, tell us a great deal about the society she lives in.

When women are confined to a singular definition of beauty, it's not only our body that is at risk of being controlled, our mind is at risk of being ensnared too.

From an early age, women are socialised to believe that we need to look a certain way to be accepted and that our value is synonymous with size.

You are more than a number. You are not your weight, your bra size, the size of your clothes, the number of calories you burn, your height, your hips-to-waist ratio, your age, the size of your appetite, your BMI, your shoe size or the number of kilos you've gained or lost. Your worth cannot be negotiated, debated or measured.

Reclaiming Your Body

❝

And I said to my body, softly. 'I want to be your friend.' It took a long breath and replied, 'I have been waiting my whole life for this.'

- Nayyirah Waheed

Reclaiming Your Body

It also probably won't surprise you that according to the good mother myth, the appearance of a mother's body reflects her competence as a mother. In other words, how a mother looks and how swiftly she bounces back to her pre-pregnancy body is an indicator of how well she is coping as a mother.

The idea of bouncing back to societal beauty standards completely ignores our metamorphosis. It muzzles the enlightenment we have gained, the aliveness we've contained, the suffering we endured and the hard work mothering requires.

Prioritising the appearance of the female body seeks to silence what a woman's body experiences and the power it possesses.

Reclaiming Your Body

For most of our life, our body has been measured on a scale of thinness, beauty and sexual desirability. Becoming a mother thrusts us into a place where these ideals can feel unrealistic and inapplicable.

The incompatibility between our maternal experiences of pregnancy, birthing, breastfeeding, mothering and the sexually objectified stereotypes of MILF and Yummy Mummy can prompt us to not only question society's narrow views of our body, but to completely reject them.

By liberating our body from society's narrow definitions, we hold the power to evoke our wildest imagination and ascribe new value and meaning to our body.

Reclaiming Your Body

Our body can feel so much more impressive and peaceful when we wash away societal ideals of thinness and sexualisation and experience it as an intricate part of nature - a wildish, life-giving force, an ecosystem to be nourished and respected, the embodiment of spirit and stardust.

Reclaiming Your Body

Be prepared. It takes time, patience and practice to perceive our body differently.

From a young age, we're socialised to understand what the female body should look like, how it should perform, how it should feel and behave.

Immersed in a highly objectified and sexualised culture, it's easy to learn how to use our body to please others, how to dress, behave, smile, pose, fake orgasm... and we probably learn all this before we learn about the anatomy of the body we live in.

The vulva, clitoris, ovaries, labia, menses, cervix, uterus - these words are more likely to elicit a sense of discomfort than the ways women's bodies have been controlled and socially constructed.

Reclaiming Your Body

Whose Body is This?

It's no surprise that the good mother myth dictates how mothers should use their body. According to the myth, the body of the good mother should be entirely devoted to caregiving.

From conception to birth, breastfeeding, midnight wakeups, constant carrying, playing, soothing, responding to sickness and resettling, the good mother is expected to happily make her body available. Even if it means sacrificing her basic needs and her well-being in the process.

Reclaiming Your Body

It's fanciful to think the aptly covered, pure, non-sexual nature of the good mother archetype, who exists for her children, will afford us a little space and sanctuary.

Within the home, as wives and partners, we are still expected to exude desirability, to partake, fulfil and experience sexual desire as if nothing has changed.

Reclaiming Your Body

For many women, it can feel as though the demands placed on our body have doubled, but our identity and our psyche have been split.

Reclaiming Your Body

Our sensuality and sexual needs, although a staple part of the good wife, must exist within certain confines.

A woman's sexual nature and reproductive ability are also seen as a threat to the destruction of the family unit, a risk to the foundation of society.

The untamed, sensual temptress is a She Monster. Can she be trusted? How can she be a good mother? Can she manage her urges, her body? Is she competent enough to manage decisions about her own body?

Society suggests not.

Reclaiming Your Body

❞

The body has been made so problematic for women that it has often seemed easier to shrug it off and travel as a disembodied spirit.

- Adrienne Rich

Reclaiming Your Body

Reconciling our sexual identity and the relationship we have with our body is layered and complex. Neither of the dominant narratives, the MILF or the good mother consider a woman's sexual energy or the needs of her body.

Instead, both objectify the maternal body as a resource for others.

Recognising our self as separate from these constructs allows us to begin deeply attuning to our body, its needs and desires.

Reclaiming Your Body

The needs and desires of our body are deeply intertwined with our sensory arousal. When our sensory system is taxed heavily it influences our effervescence, our cognitive dreaming, our psyche, our sexual and spiritual energy.

A woman's sensory system is sacred. It can easily be depleted, suffocated by the demands placed on her.

Reclaiming Your Body

Often it's the physical, emotional, social and cognitive demands placed on us and how we feel them within our body that eventually makes us crack.

It's the sensory overload of being the default parent, feeling touched out and yet remaining available to our children and our partner, the pressure to have our body look, feel, act and behave in a certain way, the need to be in two places at once, the mental exhaustion of talking to two people at once, the physical exhaustion of waking up over and over, late nights, early mornings - it's all of this, and then having to hide it behind a warm loving radiance, that often makes us crack.

Reclaiming Your Body

The lack of autonomy, agency and authority over our body urges us to look beyond the masks of motherhood and womanhood and ask, 'Whose body is this?'

This questioning marks a radical shift in the relationship we have with our body.

Reclaiming Sovereignty

Although many women feel a shift in the relationship they have with their body during matrescence, it's not always easy to articulate all the layers and shades of this change within a culture that is heavily focused on impossible standards of beauty and objectification.

Our shared understanding of the good mother myth allows us to challenge unhealthy norms and bring a woman's relationships with her body in from the periphery. It allows us to contemplate how every dimension of our reproductive identity - menses, conception, pregnancy, birthing, mothering, motherhood, matrescence, menopause - impacts the relationship we have with our body.

Reclaiming Your Body

As a mum, you'll hear a lot of talk about getting your body back, getting back to your old self, getting back into routine and back to 'normal'. Amid the pressure to return to 'normal', take time to consider which parts of normal you're going to accept into your life.

Reclaiming Your Body

Getting our body back is less about weight loss and more about reclaiming the sovereignty of our body.

Reclaiming Your Body

The processes we go through to reclaim our body and redefine the social relationships our body holds are not straightforward. But one thing is certain - matrescence gifts us the latitude to experience and perceive our body in a whole new way.

With every passing year, it becomes clearer that societal ideals of beauty, thinness and sexualisation are of little use to us, or our children when compared to the strength, power and liberation that arise from our transformative journey.

Reclaiming Your Body

The newfound perspectives that we gain as mothers can affirm a deep respect for our body, and possibly for the first time, allow us to assert true sovereignty over it.

Sovereignty over our body means confidently asserting our boundaries, renegotiating the social relationships our body conducts, respecting our embodied experiences and honouring what our body is communicating.

Sovereignty means reclaiming our body for our self.

This act of rebellion and reclamation is a radical affirmation of our autonomy and self-worth. It allows us to live fully in our body and be guided by our desires and needs, rather than expectations.

Reclaiming Your Body

When society truly recognises a woman's bodily sovereignty, it will seek to understand how trauma, social conditioning, the myths of motherhood, shifting identity boundaries and mutuality influence a woman's maternal experiences and the relationship she has with her body. It means the whole gloriously complex woman will be seen, not just her body.

> This is it: This body is home. This is where I live and hang my hat. This is where I settle into my hips and sit easy in myself, slung together with strong muscles and bones, made gentle and forging with flesh. This body is durable, has lasted for years, hunkered down through fierce storms and allows for the peaceful erosions of age. It is like a cottage on the shore: weathered and well made, a place where a person could comfortably live. I like it here. It is my own.

— Marya Hornbacher

Reclaiming Your Body

As you journey through motherhood and matrescence, remember that your body is not a resource to be exhausted, a commodity or a trend. She is not a number, a vessel, an image or an object to be possessed and assessed.

Your body is an ecosystem teeming with energy and wisdom, a labyrinth of intricately woven systems and connections. A multilingual communicator, stardust reincarnate, a vibrant force of lineage and life.

Your body is an experience. She is how you feel the sunshine on your shoulders, the sweetness of chocolate, the grass underneath your feet, and a tiny hand reaching for yours. She is the home of your soul, guiding you through the journey of life.

Celebrating Your Mother Tribe

Celebrating Your Mother Tribe

Female friendships offer a unique sanctuary, a space to be our self beyond the roles we occupy.

The friendships we cherish the most are often the ones that not only champion our mothering efforts but remind us that we must also belong to our self.

Celebrating Your Mother Tribe

Finding our tribe isn't always easy.

Forming new friendships and maintaining old ones can feel impossible amidst the juggle of work commitments, childcare and school, family schedules and illnesses. Many mothers struggle with loneliness, isolation and the complexities of socialising with young children.

You are not alone in these experiences.

Celebrating Your Mother Tribe

Historically, women's friendships have been portrayed as bitchy and competitive. These portrayals rely on a cultural narrative that women are competitors rather than collaborators.

Stereotypes such as the bitch, temptress, mean girl, super-woman, mother-in-law, wicked stepmother, the gossip, the good wife and career woman all have a remarkable ability to pit women against one another in the workplace, in relationships, and in family and social settings.

Celebrating Your Mother Tribe

The good mother myth is no exception. It informs us how good mothers should look, behave and feel, what they should prioritise, where they should be and where they shouldn't.

As a result of this socialisation, we hold our self and other mothers to impossible standards. At some point, we'll likely find our self judging and being judged by other mothers.

When we're judged on how closely we embody the look, lifestyle, behaviour, and sentiments of the good mother, it not only reinforces the 'rules' and upholds the myths – it also erodes the connections between women. It divides us. It prevents opportunity for understanding, for connection, collaboration, community, and unity.

If we let it.

Celebrating Your Mother Tribe

Finding our tribe in the jungle of motherhood is hard.

Where you can, in whatever way you can, be around other mothers, include them, connect with them. Some connections may be for a day, others a season. Others, if we're lucky, a lifetime.

Celebrating Your Mother Tribe

The female friendships that work often exude *freudenfreude* - a genuine rejoicing in another's success.

It's not always easy to embrace, or pronounce, *freudenfreude*. We're socialised to see the success of other mothers and their children as a sign that we're not doing enough - that we are not enough.

When we come to realise that 'success' is seasonal and that at some point every mother struggles to break through the same system of patriarchal motherhood - we can begin to celebrate the success of other women more genuinely.

Her success is our success.

Celebrating Your Mother Tribe

99

It turns out, one of the most wonderful joys of motherhood is the other mothers.

- Anna Jordan

Celebrating Your Mother Tribe

The tribe of women that you travel through motherhood with will be one of your greatest sources of strength.

On the days you're swimming against the tide, your friendships will sustain you. These are the women who will love you, push you, understand you, need you, celebrate you, call you out, inspire you, strengthen you, catch you and remind you that you are worthy of everything you dare to dream.

Celebrating Your Mother Tribe

The company of other mothers has a transformative and nourishing essence. Immerse yourself in its powerful alchemy.

Celebrating Your Mother Tribe

You are not meant to mother alone.

It's invaluable to spend time with people who you resonate with, who are with you in the laughter and in the silence, who encourage you and who see the best in you.

These are the people who will allow your authentic self to emerge. Open. Safe. Unfiltered.

When you feel comfortable and accepted, when you feel deeply understood and safe seeking to understand the experiences of another, real emotional nourishment and connection occurs.

This is the heartbeat of a mother tribe.

Celebrating Your Mother Tribe

It takes much too long for most of us to realise that identifying as a mother means we belong to an incredibly powerful collective of women.

Celebrating Your Mother Tribe

Together, we are embracing a newfound respect for our body, mastering new skills and a language of unconditional love, rediscovering self-worth, managing invisible burdens and shifting relationship dynamics - all while adapting to the loss of an identity and the emergence of a new one.

Together, we are changing the value of mothering.

Together, we are powerful.

Celebrating Your Mother Tribe

Despite different cultures, languages and social circumstances, mothers form a global network of ancient wisdom, stories and connections. A network with a shared understanding of humanity.

We are the healers, the weavers of peace and future traditions. We are the advocates for social change and equality.

Celebrating Your Mother Tribe

There is a bittersweet beauty in the way mothers use their agency to support and advocate for each other.

The inequalities that mothers face at home and in the workplace, locally and globally, coupled with the invisibility of mothering and matrescence, can stir within us all a belief that mothers deserve better.

This belief unites us and strengthens our collective desire to improve the systems and the culture in which we raise our children.

Celebrating Your Mother Tribe

"

Motherhood was the great equaliser for me; I started to identify with everybody ... as a mother, you have that impulse to wish that no child should ever be hurt, or abused, or go hungry, or not have opportunities in life.

– Annie Lennox

Celebrating Your Mother Tribe

Each mother tribe and generation of mothers should be celebrated.

As they build on the progress of the mothers before them, they're continuing to challenge gender norms, revolutionise parenting and bring awareness to the value of care work.

Celebrating Your Mother Tribe

Perhaps, one day, a generation of mothers will wonder what on earth we had our knickers in such a twist about. Until then, celebrate yourself - the mutuality you have with your children, your mothering wins, your body and your mother tribe. These are just some of the treasures worth celebrating in your matricentric story.

The Power of Storytelling

The Power of Storytelling

Stories are portals to the past, the future, to each other, to our self. Stories ignite inspiration for achieving the necessary, the unimaginable and the impossible. They are the breadcrumb trails set down by other women to bring us together, to show us how to come home to our self and to remind us that we are powerful.

The Power of Storytelling

Unfortunately, many of the historical stories detailing the intricacies of motherhood and matrescence have been swaddled in silence.

These missing stories are more than facts and events. These matricentric narratives, rich with wisdom, form a legacy of intergenerational knowledge, resilience and rebellion that belongs to mothers.

The Power of Storytelling

Through the stories of mothers, rich with detail and raw emotion, we can glimpse into the reality of another lived experience, another time, another culture, another generation.

The stories of the mothers who came before us remind us of the progressive changes women have created in the private and public spheres. They remind us of triumphs, of struggles overcome, and the resilience and determination passed down through generations. These narratives illuminate a path for us as we journey through motherhood and matrescence.

The Power of Storytelling

"

The words are being spoken now, are being written down; the taboos are being broken, the masks of motherhood are cracking through.

- Adrienne Rich

The Power of Storytelling

Take the time to listen to the stories of mothers from all walks of life. Matricentric stories teach us. They motivate us. They inspire us. They bundle the painful, oppressive, hilarious, embarrassing and joyous moments into narratives that connect us to our self, our children and to each other.

They are a catalyst for compassion, social change and personal transformation.

"

When you are ready, tell your own story.

There's power in allowing yourself to be known and heard, in owning your unique story, in using your authentic voice.

- Michelle Obama

The Power of Storytelling

Your story is important.

The emotions you feel, your lived experiences, the viewpoints you hold, the memories you carry, the aspirations you nurture, the dreams you shelved, the suffering, the grief, the joy, love and gratitude - these are all important.

Telling our matricentric stories is far more powerful than we realise.

Just as becoming a mother changes a woman, women can also change motherhood, not only for this generation, but for the next.

The Power of Storytelling

As our own story of motherhood and matrescence transpires, a likely feature will be the impossible social expectations of motherhood: the way we acquiesced to them and the ways they stretched and broke us.

But as our story evolves, we'll also see the rising of our feminine warrior who rebelled and rallied against expectations and biases and continued weaving love and meaningful rituals through the generations of her family.

Often, it's through our own matricentric stories that we begin to see our self differently.

The Power of Storytelling

99

To see that your life is a story while you're in the middle of living it may be a help to living it well.

- Ursula Le Guin

The Power of Storytelling

A mother's story is rarely a seamless tale of peace and perfection saturated in pastel hues and lullabies.

More commonly, it's discontentment with the status quo - swirls of confusion, chaos or anger intertwined with the love that we have for our children and our self that introduces an unexpected twist in the plot, compelling us to reclaim our voice and assert our agency to create our own liberated version of motherhood and matrescence.

Your story is yours to write. How do you imagine it?

The Power of Storytelling

If your journey through motherhood and matrescence was a story, how would it read? Are there chapters you'd like to tear out or words you wish were never spoken? Are there moments too wondrously potent to articulate?

Within this narrative, consider the burdens you encountered - the moments of self-doubt, societal expectations and the losses you faced. Intricately woven between are treasures - profound connections, mutuality, sovereignty of our body, new perspectives, and the indescribable beauty of watching life unfold.

It's the richness of your story, the delicate fusion of magic and misery, that reveals how you've evolved on your journey through motherhood and matrescence.

The Power of Storytelling

As your story unfolds, perhaps the most important questions are: whose rules do you want to live by? How do you want to feel as you craft this chapter of your life?

What sentiments do you want to feel when, years later, you reminisce and reflect on your mothering and matrescence?

Matrescence captures an intricate story of disorientation and reorientation. It depicts a mother navigating an unfamiliar terrain. Striving to discover her path and determine which aspects of herself to carry into the future, she must first see herself as an oracle of wisdom - the owner of her own life.

Even though the details may change, in each rendition of this story, in the end, it is always the mother who emerges as the heroine of her own life.

The Power of Storytelling

When our unique story comes to an end, perhaps the greatest privileges will have been, not only to make the path easier for the next generation but to have been loved by our children, to love them and to learn to love our self again in the process.

The Power of Storytelling

You've come to the end of this guidebook, but to the beginning of a new chapter in your own life.

As you journey forward, I hope the words and wisdom you found here continue to resonate. Let them serve as a reminder that you are important, you are valued, you are heard, and you are not alone.

May you navigate tough terrain with support and find sacred treasures that bring love, lightness and laughter to you and your tribe.

Stay curious.

Much love,

www.ingramcontent.com/pod-product-compliance
Lightning Source LLC
Chambersburg PA
CBHW071227070526
44583CB00017B/2082